Hidden Dimensions of Work

Hidden Dimensions of Work

Revisiting The Chicago School Methods of
Everett Hughes and Anselm Strauss

Edward B. Davis, PhD

Library of Congress Control Number: 2011905485
ISBN: Hardcover   978-1-4628-5323-6
                   Softcover   978-1-4628-5322-9
                   Ebook   978-1-4628-5324-3

This book was printed in the United States of America.

To order additional copies of this book, contact:
Xlibris Corporation
1-888-795-4274
www.Xlibris.com
Orders@Xlibris.com
76471

Contents

This book is dedicated to my son Patrick Davis and our mutual friend Shoko Maeshiro of Okinawa, Japan.

Preface

I had the great privilege of having Everett Hughes chair my dissertation committee at Boston College, and for eight years, we corresponded from my home in California and his office in Chestnut Hill. I have kept those letters and still get insights into his thinking every time I have reread them. Of course, this is true whenever I read any of his papers. His insight into society was so profound that his ideas are still fresh and exciting today. Rereading his "Humble and the Proud" paper is what prompted me to write this book. I have no delusion that my writing can be compared with Everett's, but I think that he was a marvelous teacher who instilled in me the perspective that shaped the papers, which are contained in this volume. I wrote them for him, and even though he read only four of them, I still wrote the others as if he would be viewing them. I continue to do that today even though he passed away in 1982. It is a habit—I don't think I will ever lose.

There was another event that helped get this project underway, and it, too, is related to my knowing Everett Hughes. My correspondence with Everett through my graduate career (Yes, I thought it would be a life-long event at one point) was inspired in many ways through my discussions with Anselm Strauss in San Francisco. His death in 1996 made me realize that these two gentlemen have contributed so much to our understanding of how things get done at work and the importance of knowing why this is important. Their relationship began in Chicago, was immortalized in Kansas with the *Boys in White* study, and rekindled once again when I put them together as my committee members. Anselm was never officially on my committee, but since I took classes with him (at the University of California at San Francisco after completing my exams at Boston College in 1973), I was able to discuss my research on hospitals during the next several years, and his perspective shaped the direction and style of my writing. Anselm's style was very evident in my final product, and Everett was not that happy with my adopting his perspective and language. Everett's main objection was the language of grounded theory, not what was discovered in the process of the research. They met again for the last time at the 1978 American Sociological Association meetings in San Francisco, where we sat in the Hilton mezzanine and discussed my dissertation and how they could finally make me cough it up. Trying to please them both was one of my problems (I had many in this project). It made me realize that I had to find my own voice and my own perspective, and they wanted to push me from the nest. Like most nests, it was comfortable. Having two great men who were giants in the field of sociology was enough to keep me a student for as long as I could keep the dissertation unfinished. I didn't want to be the traditional academic who became a teacher with their own students in some obscure department somewhere when I could remain a student with two of the greatest minds in sociology.

I have never had graduate students to work with and realize this is what has been missing from my work. Having undergraduates is exciting, but it is at the graduate level when one has contact with research that can inspire one to write. Of course, I'm still inspired with all of the sociology I now have the ability to see around me and am inspired still by knowing that even Robert Park didn't start writing sociology until he was fifty, having spent the first part of his life as a journalist. So now, with the passing of both Anselm and Everett, I realize that it's time to publish what I have written about work from my perspective—a perspective that has been shaped by Everett Hughes, Anselm Strauss, and the Chicago methodological tradition. If you see something in this collection of papers on work that you think is interesting, or even profound, please credit the team of Hughes and Strauss. On the other hand, if you see flaws and weaknesses, you can blame them directly on me, for I wouldn't want you to think I had bad teachers.

Introduction

Before I explain the organization of the book, I would like to explain why I study work in the first place. I had the opportunity of growing up in a very small northern California town in a place where my grandfather was born in 1871. Since the town was less than two thousand people, many even knew my grandfather and great-grandfather; I was welcomed as a child to walk into any store and business and just talk. This was in the 1950s—long before insurance companies controlled the movement of people in the workplace. I did most of my visiting during the summer when everyone was busy or during the winter holidays when things were slow for me. So I was able to view a variety of work at a very early age.

I was also fortunate in being able to enter the world of work as a wage earner about the age of eight. My first real job was working for my grandmother. My brother and I were her only grandchildren, so she was always looking for ways to slip us money. One way she could do this was to put us to work. Since my brother never had a desire to earn as much money as I did, most of the work came my way. My first regular job would be classified as a "chore" if we lived on a farm since it was related to animals. My grandmother was an entrepreneur of sorts, and one of the things that were popular during the 1950s was raising parakeets and canaries and selling them to pet stores. My grandmother had two big cages built in her backyard, and she filled one with parakeets and the other with canaries. My job was to keep the cages clean, set up the breeding boxes twice a year, and feed and water the entire bunch. I don't recall what I was paid, but every time I went up to the store to buy my grandmother Pall Malls, she would always give me an additional two dollars for myself. I continued this for a number of years even after the bottom dropped out of the bird business and the breeding boxes were put away forever.

My early observations of people at work included a close look at the newspaper business in a small town. The two Linotype machines were always a fascination to me since the melted lead at the back of the machines was transported to a place in the machinery where the letters were transposed backward and placed into the editing box so a copy could be taken prior to the type being moved into the press. If the copy was faulty, the line of type was removed, and I selected this part of the process to volunteer for whenever I was in the shop. The faulty type had to be recycled, and I slipped them into the hot lead at the back of the machine. I was probably in the fourth grade when I started my observations and continued them until I had my first girlfriend in the eighth grade and forgot all about my youthful observations.

In addition to the newspaper shop, I was also a frequent visitor to the old blacksmith shop, the library, the train station, and the city maintenance shop, where my father worked. The blacksmith shop had made the transition to a welding business back in the 1920s and 1930s, but all the tools from the horseshoeing days were still in place, and George, the owner, would build me a fire in the coal, start the electric billows, and go off to repair the farm equipment. It was then that I would place a piece of old scrap iron into the fire until it was cherry red, almost white in fact, and then take it to the anvil to shape it with the various hammers. It was the smell of the fire that I still remember and the smell of the hot metal after I plunged it into the water barrel. The four or five summers passed this way until I turned twelve and made a dollar an hour, flagging for a crop-dusting company. That was the beginning of my working-class days.

Up to that point, I was an aviary attendant, gardener (mowing lawns for two bucks apiece), and an observer of work. The flagging job was the first time I received a check. Shortly after this, I bought a new pair of work boots and was hired on weekends to empty drilling mud off railroad cars in one-hundred-pound sacks. The job consisted of lifting the sacks from one pallet to another since the forklift couldn't get into the car until the middle of the car was cleaned out. I was paid by check and earned every penny of the $2 per hour. I became quite strong doing this on weekends and was very proud of my steel-toed work boots.

Each summer after that seemed to bring a new occupation with it. I drove my first car at twelve, working for a government surveyor. He introduced me to trigonometry and geometry, and even if the work was only three weeks, I received my first experience as a surveyor's assistant. During high school, I worked as a bagger and stacker of cans in a grocery store, gas station attendant, bagger of ice at the local icehouse, and drive-in theater employee where I engaged in three separate occupations: windshield cleaner—lots of bugs on summer evenings would turn the local car windshields almost black by the time they arrived at the drive-in. I'll always remember the night the Ten Commandments was featured, and I made fifty bucks in tips. In addition, I worked as a parking lot and snack bar custodian and a marquee sign changer.

At thirteen, I had driven a D6 Caterpillar, working on rice ground for a local farmer and was proud of the fact I could be called a cat skinner. By the time I finished high school, I had worked as a sheepherder, sheep rancher, baled hay, ditch tender on rice fields, orchard irrigator, almond and walnut knocker during harvest, house dismantler, and carpenter's assistant and had roofed houses and painted houses; I was a trumpet player in several local bands. I also had joined the US Naval Reserves at seventeen and considered myself a sailor as well. My undergraduate education was only sixty miles from my home, so I was able to add several other occupations to my list by the time I was twenty-two.

After completing my MA in sociology, I was accepted as a teaching fellow at Boston College and became a college instructor at the age of twenty-four. I wanted to study work with Everett Hughes and in the process became a cabdriver and funeral home assistant as well. I lived for free above Tobin's Funeral Home on Massachusetts Avenue and unloaded caskets on weekends and answered the door and telephone at night. Since that time, I have been a consultant and researcher and owned several of my own businesses; I coached a high school rugby team and spent half a year as a rice dryer operator. All in all, I have worked in fifty-five separate occupations where I was paid a salary or wages. I have probably observed about two hundred or more occupations and professions as a sociologist, working as a researcher in hospitals, painting companies, academic institutions, and the military. The observation and the study of work has been my whole life, and I never get tired of talking about it or watching others work.

Let me now explain how I organized this book. These papers are arranged chronologically as I wrote them. They all deal with different kinds of work, and each paper is written from a different perspective.

The first chapter was written in 1971 for a course on the sociology of work, occupations, and professions. Since I lived above a funeral home, I became interested in occupations related to death. I was able to observe and study the first pathologists' assistants in the United States. I have added a letter in the endnotes section of this introduction that Everett wrote for me as a graduate student when I first expressed an interest in studying morgue attendants around Boston. I'm sure it is similar to all the letters of introduction he wrote for his University of Chicago students as they went out to do their fieldwork in the various occupations around Chicago. It gives you his thoughts on why it is important to study all kinds of work, especially "unseen kinds of work."

The second chapter was written in 1979 and was used to complete a reading and research course with Everett Hughes at Boston College, which I started in 1973 right after I completed my comprehensive exams. The research was based on observations of one of my students at California State University, Hayward. He worked part-time at a parts warehouse in the Bay Area, and he was one of my first undergraduate students in my qualitative methods course. Five years later, I was able to enter the plant to do my own observations and to complete the study just before the whole thing was sold to a Japanese automobile company, and the work force changed into something quite different from the one described here.

Chapter three was written in 1980 and was given to Everett in that same year. He liked it very much. We had been discussing risk-taking as part of my dissertation research a number of times, and this paper was a spin-off of those conversations. I first began to see risk-taking in occupations when I was driving taxi for the Checker Cab Company in Boston three nights a week while attending BC. This led me to see risk-taking as a factor in medical work, and Everett encouraged me to concentrate on how risks can be shared with those around them. I also like it, for it uses Everett's concept of career. In fact, the version you read here was written to reintroduce the concept to another generation of sociologists. I prepared it as a journal article in 1994 but never got around to sending it.

Chapter four is a paper I prepared for the 1984 ASA meetings in San Antonio, Texas—a session Anselm Strauss organized. This is my favorite, for I think the concept of work-around is important in explaining how work gets done, even though Curt Tausky disagreed with me on this subject when I sent it in as a journal article to **Work and Occupations** *in 1989*. He was the editor then, and Lee Broudy was on the editorial board. Lee worked down the hall from me at SUNY Fredonia and was instrumental in getting me hired as a visiting assistant professor because of my work with Anselm and Everett. Lee was a graduate from the University of Chicago and knew them both. He used their books in his sociology of work course, and I learned more about Chicago sociology the two years I taught there. I showed Lee the letter I wrote to Tausky after he rejected it for publication, and he thought it to be a little strong. I wonder if Curt remembers this.

Chapter five is a revised version of the last chapter in my dissertation; that work I finally did cough up for Hughes and Strauss in the end. You will be able to see Strauss's influence in this very clearly. I fought my committee at Boston College to retain this chapter since it did reflect Strauss' perspective, and it shows how the concept of the information-assessment process can be broadly applied.

Chapter six is one that I have written for this book. It is about the kind of work I did for a number of years while being a professional graduate student and when I was between my work as a sociology teacher in the California State University system or doing research in Elihu Gerson's firm, Pragmatica Systems. I always wanted to do a paper on house painters since I had such extensive experience in that work, but I just never could get a handle on it. I finally did start seeing how such a paper could be written, but I never bothered to go beyond my fieldnotes with it. Each time I drifted back into painting work, I would collect notes from the urban artist's perspective and put them away again when I found a "real" job—teaching or organizational consulting. I spent so much time painting over the years; I even obtained my painting contractor's license. I even used it for a while after my research tour of India depleted my bank account. I think it is also interesting that my training with Emil Zollinger helped shape the urban artist's perspective.

Emil is a Swiss citizen who has lived and worked in San Francisco since 1963 as a painting contractor. His apprenticeship in Zurich was a traditional one for a young man wishing to learn the painting craft. His teacher was a fellow who used his fists on occasion to emphasize a point—a teaching method quite common with the trades in Europe. Emil never struck his painters, but he was a taskmaster who was able to make artists of us all. He always amazed me with his talent and his love of the profession that he defended with a Swiss passion. He always wanted me to be his foreman, but since I was always employed so sporadically with him over the years, I was never able to perform this role. He was always willing to hire me when I needed the work, and I am grateful to him for keeping food on my table on many occasions. This chapter is really dedicated to him.

Chapter seven is about work I have done for almost twenty years now—academic administration. Everett once wrote an article called "Teaching as Fieldwork." I thought mine should be quite similar. I wrote it while I was still working for what I call Overseas American University in Asia. I was also inspired by Andrew Abbott's work on professions at the time and thought it might be interesting to contemplate what we are doing to ourselves as a profession.

Chapter eight is a paper I wrote for the ASA meetings in New York in 1996. My research on illusion construction has been inspired not only by Hughes and Strauss and their comments concerning the hidden dimensions of society but also by Georg Simmel and his thinking on the secret. It is still about work in a way since it takes work to construct the illusions we create around us.

I hope you enjoy reading about the work I have had the pleasure to observe.

The Chicago Tradition

The series of papers contained in this volume are projects that I wrote between 1971 and 1996. I wrote the early ones for my graduate work at Boston College and the later ones for either an American Sociological Association session or my own satisfaction. None of the papers have been published, but all represent the qualitative approach known as the Chicago school or Chicago tradition. Another purpose in writing this introduction is to comment on why the Chicago school perspective has been so important in shaping the qualitative sociology that has emerged from its influence.

For decades now, books and articles about Chicago school sociology have been written in an attempt to chronicle and describe its origins and its impact on American sociology in general. Many authors have attempted to interpret what made the Chicago tradition so unique—beginning with Robert E. L. Faris's work, *Chicago Sociology: 1920-1932,* published in 1967, and ending with the most recent 1999 book by Andrew Abbott, *Department and Discipline: Chicago Sociology at One Hundred.* Abbott devotes much of his first chapter to those authors who began to critique and interpret what the Chicago school represented.

The essence of this sociological perspective is that one cannot just do library research but must go into the field to collect data. The University of Chicago department was a joint department into the 1930s with anthropology—a discipline that Boas shaped in America by also demanding field research. Everett Hughes always insisted on spending at least two years in the field before completing a research project. It took me over six years to patch together twenty-four months of observations for my dissertation. The first chapter of this book represents a year of observations in Boston hospitals but only about ninety days of actual fieldwork over a twelve-month period. In addition to the lengthy stays in the field, the Chicago school was identified by the use of comparative analysis. Being able to make comparisons with a variety of other sources was another requirement of Everett's students.[1] Andrew Abbott is perhaps one of the more significant and contemporary defenders of the Chicago tradition and is a big advocate of returning to such a research tradition and the excitement of fieldwork. "We have given up writing about the real world, hiding in stylized worlds of survey variables, historical forces and theoretical abstractions . . . In a single sentence, the Chicago school thought—and thinks—that one cannot understand social life without understanding the arrangements of particular social actors in particular social times and places."[2] This, in essence, is what the Chicago school was—and I like this about Abbott's use of the present tense in the previous quote (is)—all about. It was what Hughes and Strauss taught their students all of their lives—to be faithful to the real world.

This introduction to the intimate details of what made the Chicago school tick was provided to us by Andrew Abbott's wonderful research project that is contained in his book *Department and Discipline: Chicago Sociology at One Hundred.* From Abbott's book, we learn early on that the department of the 1920s, 1930s, and up through the 1950s was a department made of varying personalities. "Hauser, Blumer, Wirth, Janowitz: these were men who made many people—including some of their colleagues—very uncomfortable. Sometimes irascible and contemptuous, always committed and brilliant, they had little time for those without their passions and talents, and very little inclination to hide that opinion. Others were more courtly and gracious; this was the public character of such men as Small, Burgess, and Hughes."[3] One can make this same claim concerning Anselm. Kind, gentle, and brilliant was his legacy to all of his students. So I had the pleasure of dealing with gentlemen in the strictest sense.

But what confused me about Abbott's book was the conflict that occurred between Blumer and Hughes. Knowing Everett for over ten years, I never heard one word of bitterness concerning Blumer's concept of symbolic interaction nor my use of Blumer's material in my papers and conversations. I had met Blumer only twice and then only briefly at two ASA conventions. I recall him as blustery and a man who could fill an entire room with his presence. I never once felt that way about Hughes or Strauss. But I was amused to learn from Abbott that Hughes represented the best of the "doers" while Blumer was more cautious and concerned more with making methodological mistakes than actually doing fieldwork (see Abbott's book, especially his second chapter). However, I don't think there was ever a question that Robert Park played a big role in insuring that whatever research was conducted at Chicago during his tenure, it always involved real situations with an awareness of everyday reality. All of Park's students learned this and carried on this tradition with great passion. This was the one element that they all shared but articulated in different ways.

Abbott's second chapter of *Disciplines* reveals the conflict that ensued when Park's students began to squabble over who would "replace" him and carry on his work. Abbott makes several references to the various "claimants to Park's throne" including Blumer and Wirth. At one point, Abbott writes, " . . . [Reisman] wrote that Hughes as the only heir to Park . . ."[4] and for another example, Abbott writes about a satire Hughes wrote about the history of the Chicago school:

" . . . in which Hughes shows that his views had just as fine a Chicago pedigree as anyone else's and that credentials as 'sociologists' matter little, the great figures of the department having been a Baptist economist (Small), an English professor (Thomas), a philosopher turned newspaperman (Park), and a psychologist (Faris)."[5]

Abbott continues with this thought about the satirical piece. "It must have been a real slap in the face indeed to Wirth and Blumer. For underneath its satire is the bold assertion that Hughes himself was the real inheritor of Robert Park."[6]

Abbott makes another observation concerning the divisiveness of the department during the 1950s. "The faculty was still split between quantitative and qualitative parties, although the balance inclined toward the qualitative. Warner, Hughes, Reisman, Foote, Horton, Blau, and

Strauss were qualitative in one way or another, although only Hughes and Strauss really represented old Chicago."[7] I was unaware of all of the historical conflicts that emerged from this group of sociologists, but I was aware of some of them from my conversations with Everett Hughes and Anselm Strauss during the 1970s and 1980s.

Anselm Strauss was a product of the second generation of the Chicago school and learned eventually what this tradition was all about—staying close to the field for an extended time. I say "learned eventually" since I had the opportunity to interview Anselm in the spring of 1980 about his graduate school experiences, and he provided some background on how he learned what to do with data once it was collected. The following is an excerpt from this interview that relates directly to his understanding of the Chicago tradition and how he was shaped by it.

Interview with Anselm Strauss
San Francisco, California
Spring 1980

I went to Chicago because it was the only place to go. The alternative was to go to Columbia. There were several professors I was interested in working with at Chicago. One was Louis Wirth, and the other was Blumer. When I went to Chicago, I first met Blumer, and in two weeks, he had me doing research for him, so I moved very naturally into the symbolic interactionist orbit. The other thing I remember is that he told me to go read Mead, so there, in my first weeks at Chicago—in the heat of summer—I was sweating over Mead. I had already read Park and Dewey—the Dewey book was on social psychology, and it had a great impact on me, and the other was concerning logic.

When I got to Chicago, I studied primarily with Blumer—he was my hero—but I took courses with everybody else. There was no question that I would fall out on the side of the symbolic interactionist tradition.

I have been asked what subject had the greatest impact on my graduate work. At the University of Virginia, I was a premedical student, and I took a lot of humanities and biology. The two subjects I was most involved with were sociology and psychology. And I had very good teachers in both areas. When I finished my college education, there was a question about whether I would become a psychologist or sociologist. And I think this is probably the most relevant information for you since

I could have gone in either direction. The psychologist told me that the employment prospects were very poor (this was in 1939 in the depth of the Depression). The sociologist told me that sociology was a good field, but it didn't have many Jews in it, and they didn't get very well placed. So I was faced with the prospect of two fields that I wouldn't get employed. Anyway, I decided for sociology, but this is relevant because I became a social psychologist.

The title of my masters' thesis I can't remember, but it was a library research on attitudes. I looked at the theoretical and the empirical approaches and did an analysis of what was wrong with all of that. For my doctoral thesis, I worked with Burgess who was famous for family studies, and I did a study on mate selection. I was very bored with it, and I did it to get finished because I had taken so long with my masters' thesis I just had to get out. It had one Burgess feature, which was that I discovered I was good at statistics but I didn't like it. I also did a lot of in-depth interviewing because of what Burgess was doing with qualitative data and putting statistics together. I think I should add that under Hauser, I did some side readings, but I never heard about Mead under him, which indicates that Hauser himself never had a course with Mead, which in itself is interesting because many people at Chicago were really acquainted with Mead, as Fisher and I pointed out in one of our articles in *Symbolic Interaction.*

I have also been asked to comment on what accounts for the changes in the topics of my work.

The best way to do this is to do it chronologically. When I left the University of Chicago, I was quite excited about research that Blumer had done, and he had made some suggestions in an unpublished paper. Two of the topics were daydreaming and loneliness. So when I went off to my first job to teach in 1944, I began to do research on daydreaming, and I turned out to be quite an ingenious collector of data, but I didn't know what to do with it. The same thing happened with loneliness. I did a fair amount of data collecting and simply didn't know what to do with it. And then I gradually realized that I hadn't learned at Chicago what to do with data except the statistical techniques. And I really hadn't figured it out yet, so I put that aside, and meanwhile I did a textbook on social psychology with Lindesmith and a couple of critiques of anthropological and psychological literature.

At Indiana University, I did a Piaget-like study of children in the meaning of money to them. This was between 1949 and 1952 in through there.

When I went to Chicago (to teach), two things were going on with me. I was wondering if something was lacking in me in understanding social psychology, and I did not have it very well formulated then. But my phrasing of it at the time, which eventually is better phrased in *Mirrors and Masks*, is that social psychology has to go hand-in-hand with social organizational aspects and vice versa—social organization without social psychology didn't get into the heart of interaction—and social psychology lacked something if it didn't have the organizational. That was the first important thing.

The second was when I went back to Chicago (to teach), I discovered that Everett Hughes and his students, such as Howard Becker and Erving Goffman, were working on studies of occupations and work, and that was the beginning of my empirical grounding. And I will say more about that in a moment. *Mirrors and Masks* started in the summer of 1953, and Nelson Foote was instrumental in getting me to Chicago in the autumn of 1952. Foote's idea was to put together a reader, and I was supposed to do the section on social psychology. So during the summer of 1953, I sent down about the first-third of what was to become *Mirrors and Masks*. That section was hectographed—that was the process before xeroxing—you could get an alternative of either getting a manuscript mimeographed or hectographed, which was a pale purple. Anyway, that was called an "essay on identification." It circulated among the graduate students for the next two and a half years and was a fairly popular reading in the social psychology classes that I taught. Then what happened was that Foote's book never came to fruition. No one did anything on their segment, and I wasn't finished, and I wasn't going to finish it until the work was done by the other people.

In the fall of 1955, I went to Frankfurt on an exchange professorship, and I was there for four or five months, and I was doing interviews of German city planners and studying the rebuilding, which was part of my research on urban relations. When I got back to the United States in late March of 1956, I found that my subliminal processes had been working away. In fact, I was very eager to get back the last month or two, not quite knowing why I was so eager. Not that I was tired of Germany or that I wanted to get back, but apparently something was moving inside me—a small motor maybe—and so when I got back,

I finished *Mirrors and Masks* in the next three months. If you look closely at it, you begin to see that it really does flow in two parts. One is the summation of my social psychological period before I got back to Chicago in 1952, and the rest of it really is my reworking of the Everett Hughes occupational tradition—putting together social psychology and social organization—plus an historical interest, which I had also developed at Chicago, working with a social historian, whose name is Richard Wohl, now deceased.

In 1958, I left the University of Chicago at the breakup of the department (see pp. 62-79 in Abbott's book for a detailed discussion of how this occurred), and I went to a section of a hospital called the Institute for Psychosomatic and Psychiatric Research. I worked for a friend who was the assistant director, and I worked out a proposal for a project, which became eventually the book on psychiatric ideologies. I recruited two students to work with me on that book. What happened was the psychiatrist on the project had the idea of studying three psychiatric ideologies and wondering what impact that had on the care of patients. Three sociologists on the project told him to combine the sociology of work and occupations and social movements and my Meadian kind of social psychology. And out of that, as I'm sure you know, came the idea of negotiated order and the idea of arenas.

I left Chicago in 1960 and came out to California, and there I decided to do something in the field of medical sociology that would, perhaps, make a practical impact, and I wanted it to be an important study. I also felt in me the conviction that it did not make any difference what area you studied you can make sociology out of it.

I never had a course with Everett Hughes as a graduate student although I sat in on some of his classes and at the time I couldn't see that he had very much to say—not until I was back [to teach in 1952] when I was on the faculty, until I really learned what I had really missed because I think he was one of the best sociologists America has ever produced. Anyway, the sociology I brought to the UCSF [University of California San Francisco] studies on dying and chronic illness and grounded theory was based upon the model of Everett Hughes.*

*Emphasis is mine.

The Everett Hughes Model

Anselm lays out very nicely what he called the Everett Hughes model, but this emphasis of looking at organizations from a social psychological perspective was recognized by Robert E. L. Faris in his book, *Chicago Sociology: 1920-1932*, which was published in 1967.

"Park, busy with other subjects, nevertheless was sensitive to the importance of the study of organization and stimulated it as the opportunity became available. His student and close friend Everett Hughes later became a principle developer at Chicago of this direction of interest . . . This interest led him into a long career of studying organization in general and a variety of specific organizations and the processes within them. In the course of these studies, Hughes provided apprenticeship, training, and stimulation to a large number of younger students who also became productive in this area of sociology."[8]

Since organizations are generally places where people work, this was a logical area for Hughes to concentrate upon and where interactions could be observed, and sociology could emerge in a variety of ways. In understanding how people interact at work, or with the workers in the case of patients or clients, we gain insight into how meaning, or definition of the situation, gets defined. How does work get defined? Who does what kind of work and how do the rules of work get made, get interpreted, and get redefined as people in the work organization go about their day? [9]

Work organizations can give us a unique view of the larger society by allowing the sociologist to address and observe how people deal with social control in their lives. Robert Park's influence in shaping the Chicago school of sociology was his focus on the various ways society can attempt to control our behaviors. The study of work gives us the window of viewing how social control works and allows the sociologist to understand not only the obvious means of control but also the various ways people can escape from these formal control processes in overt and covert ways. In observing people at work, we can learn how people can construct their social worlds, how they can maintain them, and how they live within the confines of these unique social arrangements for extended periods of time.

The Chicago school methodologies and symbolic interactionist perspective allow the sociologist to get close enough to paint an accurate picture of what may be transpiring within a society—to the point where even the hidden aspects of our behaviors can be identified and described with some accuracy.

I believe it is the hidden behaviors that reveal much of how a society works, and I also believe that the Chicago school has been able to allow its sociologists to focus on these behaviors and succeed in capturing how hidden behaviors work. The following passage by Everett Hughes provides us a nice summary of why hidden behaviors need to be catalogued and described even though it may be difficult to do so. This particular paragraph has never been published since it was discovered by Howard London, one of Everett's students, tasked with filing his material after his death in 1982. Howard and I shared our graduate careers at Boston College with Everett, and he showed me this writing in 1996 many years after he discovered it. After I read it, which Howard had conspicuously displayed in his office, he asked me, "Now doesn't that sound just like Hughes and what he was interested in?" I had to agree, and I'm delighted to share it with the readers here.

Sociology

Is there some sound barrier of knowledge beyond which, if people continue and accelerate their inquiries and applications, we shall be blown up physically and morally? If so, physical, not social knowledge will be our undoing. The most we can, with our knowledge of ourselves, would be to hoist us on a small Fourth of July petard. As a matter of fact, humans are not at all sure how much they want to know about other people, themselves included and especially. We spy upon one another, while hiding our own skeletons and campaign plans; or we declare that we will be frank, and mean that some bit of frankness will conceal a many times larger iceberg of secrecy. Some of us learn some wisdom, based on self-knowledge and well-analyzed experience of others, and then forget it, as a favor to our egos or interests; and, if we do not so forget it, we are such ineffective teachers that the next generation does not or will not learn it from us, and must blunder along—or worse, since with one good solution ruled out because their elders used it, they have less chance of finding the right one. Some things, once learned by people, stay learnt. So it seems with mathematics, physics and the like.

Other things, perhaps intellectually easier to learn, are less likely to be learnt at all, and run a great risk of being socially forgotten. Sociology seeks precisely that kind of knowledge which is most easily forgotten, and about which people are most sensitive.

Everett C. Hughes
Found in Professor Hughes' Boston
College office by Howard London in 1983.

Keep in mind that Park was significantly influenced by Georg Simmel, and it was Simmel who first wrote about the importance of the secret in society. In many ways, I believe the methods and the symbolic interactionist perspective, which emerged from the Chicago school, are attempts to capture the secret or hidden behaviors that make society work. We can see this clearly when we spend time, watching people work. Many of the important things that occur in a work organization have a hidden quality to them among those who do the work. You will see this at various times in the chapters contained in this volume. You will see this especially in the last chapter since it is an attempt to expand upon why sociologists should consider "the hidden" as an important pipeline into the machinations of society. Everywhere sociologists turn, they are confronted with roadblocks, dead-ins, and stonewalling when conducting research. For various reasons (lack of funding being the primary one), we do what we can to complete the research and move on. But it is the hidden, the attempt to hide, and the divulging of secrets that can explain much of the sociology we seek. Many times people will construct elaborate illusions to contain the hidden information that Hughes was thinking about in his above quote. It is the illusion constructions that may be the most interesting focus for sociologists today.

Chapter One

On the Fringes of Medicine: From Diener to Pathologists' Assistant

A Social Psychological Investigation of a New Paramedical Career

Davis, I think you will become a sociologist.
—Everett Hughes

This was the message I received on a handwritten note attached to this paper when it was returned to me after being graded by Dr. Hughes. I completed this paper for Sociology 260 at Boston College—Work, Occupations, and Professions—and the beginning of my study of work as a sociologist.

Also, see the endnotes for Chapter One to see the letter of introduction Dr. Hughes provided me for this research project.

Before one can be on the fringes of anything, there must first be a central entity from which the fringe is attached. The entity in this case is the large esoteric body of knowledge known to Western man as scientific medicine; the fringe to which I refer is the morgue attendant or diener. This particular "fringe" in medicine has been "hanging" from the medical fabric long before medicine established a strong monopoly in the sick-role process. The word *diener* comes from the German influence on medicine and means servant. The duty he performs in the autopsy suite and other areas in the department of pathology certainly makes him a servant of the physician with all of the prestige that surrounds any servant role.

During the course of this study, I have noticed varying degrees of diener roles in four different hospital settings. Each role is dependent upon the work setting one finds himself in plus the experience the diener has incorporated while working with pathologists. Basically, there are three major types of dieners that have been utilized by the medical profession during the course of my observations. However, I have devoted an entire section to a fourth diener type, which has just emerged during the last year. I discovered such a "type" while researching the role of diener in various hospitals in New England, and at the time of this writing (spring 1971), there are only three such "types" in medicine today. Although this fourth category of diener is not considered a diener within the medical field, he comes closest to such a term in a sociological sense. For example, the first type of diener I have classified I call the "traditional German diener." He is quite similar to the German diener who was trained to do a complete "gross autopsy" by the physicians. The fourth diener type is called a pathologists' assistant and is also trained to do a complete "gross autopsy" plus the clinical and microscopic work as well. In this respect, the pathologists' assistant is a new emerging role in medicine that is attempting to stand between the diener and the pathologist himself. One of the main concerns of this study is the examination of the identity of the diener and the pathologists' assistant and all of the trouble and conflicts that ensue in this "dialectic of identities." The two diener types that stand between the "traditional" and the "pathologists' assistant" roles are the "transient diener" and the "modern diener." All four types will be discussed at length in this paper along with the social processes that shape them.

This entire study has been designed to examine a minority career that has been neglected by the field of behavioral science either as a career in paramedicine or as a position in the hierarchy of the hospital. In the process, light may be shed on some of the social psychological relationships that have occurred during the "emergent role process" of the pathologists' assistant in this struggle as an identity in medicine.

One of the main generalizations I can note in my contact with occupations of death is that death is definitely a male occupation, and the role of diener and pathologists' assistant is no exception to this rule. Another generalization that has also been quite evident to this writer is the stigma each occupation of death carries with it as one of the career contingencies.[10]

Aside the work roles, core activities, and carrier contingencies of the diener and pathologists' assistant, there is another role that must be discussed in relation to medicine prior to an examination of the fringes of that profession. I am referring to the role of pathology in general and where it fits into the sociology of the healing occupations and the hospital. It has become very apparent during the course of this study that the field of pathology has a difficult time in attracting medical students for internships and resident training. It's as if the area of pathology carries some form of stigma within the profession of medicine itself. The result of this recruitment problem has led to a transitional period for pathology where its role is not clearly defined within the profession, and as a result, the roles of the paramedical occupations surrounding pathology are also undergoing identity crises.

Some of the terminology used in this report will have to be clarified for those not versed in medical jargon. The first term that should be clarified is "pathology" itself. Obviously it means the "study of disease," but it has come to mean a number of other functions in the field of medicine besides this strict definition. The exact usage of this word will be clarified for the reader in the next few pages and subsequently throughout the entire report. There are various aspects of pathology that should be mentioned at this time also. "Anatomical pathology" refers to that area within pathology that specializes exclusively with human anatomy and all those activities centered on the organs. "Clinical pathology" is that specialized area that deals with the analysis of human tissue from the body in order to determine the degree of pathology (both normal and abnormal) in the composition of tissue. "Clinical" can also determine not only diagnosis of disease but also prognosis. Many times, the clinician asks for the advice of the pathologists for prognostic procedures.

One of the main focal points of interaction for the triadic relationship of the doctor, diener, and pathologists' assistant or the dyadic relationship between doctor/diener, diener/pathologists' assistant, or doctor/pathologists' assistant is the postmortem examination. From this point on, this procedure will be called the "post" and shall refer to both "restricted" and "non-restricted" cases. Restricted cases are those that are limited to specific organ examination only, leaving the remaining portions of the body untouched. Once there is a death in the hospital, the relatives are notified by "booking," and permission to perform the autopsy is requested.[11] From the time of death until permission is either granted or denied by family, the body is called "pending" by both booking and pathology. Once the "pending" becomes a "post," the body is given a number and is referred to on all work organization documents by this autopsy number.

There will be other terms that will be used in this report from time to time, but each will be explained more fully when they appear in the body.

A Brief View of the Role of Medicine

Before moving into the area within medicine that this study deals (pathology), it is necessary to first examine the medical profession in general. It is quite evident that most societies have some form of healing system built into the culture and directed toward the goal of health maintenance. We know that in this society and in most other Western cultures, the healing system has become institutionalized and specialized in the last sixty to seventy years to a point where it is now one of the high-status professions, at least for those working directly with scientific medicine. This institutionalization of scientific medicine has been due to a number of factors, which contribute to the high status of the physician and which will not be our concern at this time. The fact remains that the role of scientific medicine is quite stable and permits the physician to exhibit a great deal of freedom and autonomy as long as he adheres to the basic principles of the esoteric body of knowledge from which he emerged. Along with this freedom, there are costs that the doctor must accept as part of his role. One of these costs, a career contingency, which the medical practitioner must face every day, is responsibility. Becker and Hughes have pointed this out very well in *Boys in White*:

> Medical responsibility for the patient's well being, and the exercise of Medical responsibility is seen as the basic and key action of the practicing physician. The physician is most a physician when he exercises this responsibility.[12]

This responsibility means that the fate of the patient is in the hands of the physician at all times. Once this relationship has been formulated between doctor and patient, there is created a social psychological mode of social control on the part of the physician. A parallel can be made between this "giving of life" on the part of medical science and gift giving in general. Schwartz[13] has demonstrated how the gift can act as a controlling mechanism in a relationship of any kind and quotes Levi-Strauss concerning this aspect, where "goods are not only economic commodities but also vehicles and instruments for realities for another order: influence, power, sympathy, status, emotion."[14] When one is in the position to give the "gift of life," it seems reasonable that the giver becomes a powerful influence within the culture. This power situation between the giver and the receiver of life becomes even more favorable to the former because the latter is not in a position to reciprocate.

The principle of reciprocity, then, may be used as a tool in the aspiration for and protection of status and control. William F. White, for instance, notes that the leader takes care not to fall into debt to his followers, but to insure, on the contrary, that the benefits he renders unto others are never fully repaid.[15]

Such is the role of the physician. Out of this responsibility to the patient, the doctor receives a social psychological advantage that is used to legitimate his role in society.

Eliot Freidson has pointed out an important aspect of the medical profession that is pertinent to this study. He maintains that medicine is generally more concerned with applying rather than creating or contributing to science. Freidson points out that the clinician is one who must deal with patients not on a theoretical and scientific basis but on an action orientation. Because of this role as "applier of knowledge," the physician begins to rely upon his own subjective experiences. As the physician's experience grows, the reliance upon theoretical medicine becomes less and less, and those procedures that have worked for the doctor in the past became most important. This division within the medical division of labor is quite noticeable when viewing the profession from the side of pathology.

According to Hughes, each profession and/or occupation has a license to carry on certain kinds of work, which no other people are allowed to perform, and a mandate to enforce the conduct necessary to perform the licensing tasks. At this time, there is no strict licensing of one particular healing system that excludes others from applying healing knowledge even though they may not be based upon scientific standards. Because of this, one may choose to see a chiropractor, osteopath, or Christian Science healer with the same freedom as one has to make an appointment with a medical doctor. However, medical science has the exclusive license to investigate and legitimate the cause of death in this society. No other area of the healing system is permitted to deal with the dead for investigative purposes. For this reason, the role of pathology plays a very large part in medicine even though the pathologist is not in a position to obtain the same status as a clinician, working with live patients. The pathologist is generally not in a position to make crucial decisions, except in relation to surgical diagnosis, and does not have the degree of responsibility to a patient directly. Most of the responsibility of pathology lies in its scientific orientation and procedures that make it a distinct entity within medicine. Because of this unique role, there is even lower visibility to the workings of a pathologist than to a medical doctor. Because of their low visibility to the lay public and to the other various roles in medicine too, it would appear that pathology is free to establish any mandate procedures it desires to insure that its role as scientist and researcher maintains its exclusive position within scientific medicine. The next few sections will, in part, describe some of these mandate procedures that are now emerging with the pathologists' assistant role and the result these mandate procedures have had upon the role of the diener.

One of the major areas in medicine that this paper deals with is the role of paramedical positions and their relation to the medical profession. Since one of the central distinctions between an occupation and a profession according to Freidman is the concept of autonomy or "a position of legitimate control over work," it is quite apparent that a very few, if any paramedical roles now in medicine, will ever become professions upon their own. The role of paramedical workers is always being controlled by the medical profession through either the distribution of knowledge and training, i.e., the physician's approving curriculum, etc., or the establishing of mandates to control the type of tasks to be performed at the request or orders of the physician. Hughes points out that as medicine changes, the doctor begins to delegate tasks that were once an integral part of his own role, and in a sense, he creates the new paramedical positions.

> As medical technology develops and changes, particular tasks are constantly downgraded; that is, they are delegated by the physician to the nurse. The nurse in turn passes them on to the maid. But occupations and people are being upgraded, within certain limits. New workers come in at the bottom

of the hierarchy to take over the tasks abandoned by those occupations that are ascending the mobility ladder.

Others come in outside the hierarchy as new kinds of technology (photography, electronics, and physics) find a place in the medical effort. Satisfactory definitions of role for the new people are notoriously lacking in a system in which rigidly defined roles and ranks are the rule.[16]

Freidson makes an interesting point when he states that this aspect in the medical division of labor called paramedical exists only in those societies where scientific medicine is established and that it is the only profession that has imposed such strict guidelines on the occupations involved around it.[17] It is quite apparent that the role of the paramedical personnel will always be subordinate to the physician since the profession is in a position to dictate the exact tasks to be performed. The role of all paramedical occupations is to assist the physician in his duties, and because of this subordinate position, those in paramedical roles will always have lower status than the physician within the society. This does not mean that those in the paramedical role will not strive to maintain some form of identity of their own to emulate the role of physician by borrowing the same prestige symbols such as white coats or using Latin phrases at opportune times. Both the diener and the pathologists' assistant are paramedical roles that have developed around pathology, and both of these are constantly trying to establish a role identity within medicine. Both Hughes and Freidson have indicated that all paramedical positions create conflicts within the medical division of labor due to shifting technology or the insistence on the part of the physician to delegate the dirty work to new positions within medicine. This entire study concerns itself with these conflicts that occur around pathology's paramedical roles and the effect this conflict interaction has upon the role of the pathologist in general.

Even though there have been several studies that have investigated some of these paramedical conflict processes in medicine, the role of pathology has been almost entirely neglected. The only reference this writer has found is the work of Sudnow when he briefly mentioned the role of the morgue attendant in the work system within the hospital that dealt directly with death. Sudnow, however, never mentioned any role conflicts that arose between the pathologist and the paramedical positions that are associated with this branch of medicine. He also failed to mention the exact role pathology itself plays within the profession. It is hoped that some insight into these problems will be given in the following pages for the sociological processes, which are common to pathology, may also be applicable to other areas of medicine and other professions in general. One of the points that emerged from Sudnow's study is most pertinent to this paper, for he did capture the identity crises that the morgue attendant or diener has to labor under, and he did give an excellent account of the various work systems that deal with the dead patient. The most apparent role image the diener has established within the hospital is very much stigmatized. This stigma is a career contingency that is a part of every occupation that deals with death. Goffman's account of stigma indicates that symbols play a part in the disclosure of one's identity, for they become visible to the people. Sudnow's example of the morgue attendant's cart is a good illustration of Goffman's point, for everyone knew there had been a death when they witnessed the cart in the hallway. This stigma does not stop with the diener's role but affects the entire pathology department as well. It appears that any role associated with this branch of medicine is contaminated and becomes a part of the identity of the person that works in the department. This was even true with this researcher, for I found on several occasions that most people associated me with pathology and always made comments about dead bodies. Even mentioning my research topic to colleagues brought an immediate response of repulsion on their part and to some degree, placed stigma upon my own identity. This same stigma is associated with all death occupations; I had a unique position to judge this identity contingency since I lived above a funeral home and watched the eyes of the public stare as I walked to the door to unlock it. This stigma plays a major part in the diener's and pathologists' assistant's role and is one career contingency from which one cannot escape. The nurses in his own study also stigmatized Sudnow, for they would always make comments about "ghoul," meaning Sudnow.

The Diener

Now that we have some background on the relationship between paramedical careers and medicine, the role of the diener will be more easily identified and classified using the criteria previously discussed.

The general role description of the diener has changed considerably since its first introduction into medicine about one hundred years ago.

Hughes has pointed out in his examination of work that almost every occupation has some tasks that are considered the dirty work and most generally the lowest employee within the work system is obliged to perform these duties. The diener is a perfect example of this process, for he has been used by medicine exclusively for the dirty work the physician has refused to perform. All of this dirty work centers on the autopsy room in general and the "post" in particular. It is difficult to describe the autopsy procedure without going into great detail concerning the more morbid aspects. The autopsy is most definitely a gross operation and not in the anatomical senses either. It is simply gross. It is impossible to describe my feelings during the first "post" this writer witnessed, for it would involve a total list of symptoms beginning with waves of nausea and sweating palms to weak knees and cold perspiration. After about ten to fifteen minutes and a great deal of self-control, I was able to watch the procedure again without mishap. During the course of this study, I found that everyone's first "post" from dieners to doctors was quite similar to the initial period of shock that I experienced. As a diener told me, "Once you get past the first one, you're all right."

In the hospitals that were observed during this study, all had the same qualifications for diener that included some background in the field of medicine and/or experience with other occupations of death such as morticians and embalmers. I asked one of the personnel departments why it was necessary to have any background at all since the job did not require any skills to begin with. The reply to this question was most interesting, for he said, "We want someone who can work with death without getting sick."

The careers of dieners vary considerably, which the classification will illustrate a few pages from now. However, there are certain tasks that all dieners perform, which should be mentioned at this point.

Core Activity of the Diener

For the diener, there is one core activity that involves most of his time and energy and centers around the autopsy procedure. The diener, whether he be the "traditional," "modern," or "transient," must be responsible for a number of tasks, which center on the "post." In most cases, the diener is responsible for preparing the instruments that include knives, saws, syringes, string, and culture tubes. The instruments must be cleaned and available to the doctor prior to the "post." Another task of the core activity involves the moving of the body from the morgue to the autopsy room, removal of the wrapping on the body, and placement of the body on the stainless steel table. Once the body is ready, the diener is then available to the doctor as an extra set of hands during the prosection. The prosection involves the cutting and evisceration of the body by the physician except for the removal of the skullcap that is strictly a diener's job. Once the skull is removed, I have observed both the diener and the physician removing the brain, depending upon the criteria of the pathologists present. In some hospitals, the doctor always removes the brain for fear the diener is not capable of the task without damaging the tissue. In most cases, however, the diener does remove the brain and does occasionally remove the organs and intestines on his own. These particular tasks vary within pathology depending upon the workload, doctor's personality, and work system in general. After the brain and organs are removed, however, the role of diener is quite clear in all the work settings I have observed. The skullcap is rejoined with the head by the diener, the scalp is pulled from over the face where it is placed during brain removal, and it is sutured by the diener. The body is then prepared by the diener to be closed. The breastplate is rejoined, and the body cavity closed. After the sewing of the incision, the blood is washed from the body and pulled onto the gurney wheeled to the morgue, waiting the arrival of the undertaker. Most believe that death is an end in itself. That may be true biologically. However, once a death has occurred, it is only the beginning for those occupations dealing exclusively with death. As the dead body is moved out of the hospital, there is an entire work system it must confront and pass through until the flowers are placed upon the grave and estate settled through the legal system. At the present time, there has been no descriptive analysis on this work system of death occupations, and the area is ripe for study.[18]

Classification of Dieners and Career Contingencies

During the observation of this minority career of diener, I have noted recurrent patterns and career contingencies that involve four major classifications within the work system. Before these diener "types" are described and explained, there are some career contingencies that are common to all dieners in all work settings observed and should be pointed out. First of all, how does one become a diener? What are some of the turning points in the life of an individual that direct his interests to this minority career? Since the qualifications of all the hospitals specify that the diener should have some experience in the medical field or funeral business, there are some limitations on exactly who is permitted to enter the occupation. The exposure one has had with medicine does not have to be too great because some of the dieners I interviewed had only been orderlies prior to dienering. Many of the dieners interviewed have had more contact with the funeral business than with medicine, but this might have been a bias in the sample since a random procedure was not used. Since contacts have to be made to enter the funeral business,[19] some individuals use the diener job to establish such contacts in order to be recommended for enrollment with the mortuary school. There have been some dieners who have drifted into the occupation more out of necessity according to one medical examiner I interviewed. He said, "Most morgue attendants are alcoholics, sexual deviants, and unemployables." Such a comment comes from a physician who has worked with many of these people during his career in pathology since 1945. Since the occupation does carry more than its share of stigma, it stands to reason that the diener role is quite hard to fill. Such a statement by the medical examiner is still a strong indictment on the diener. During my observations, I heard of only a few cases of necrophilia on the part of the dieners in a few hospitals, and I did not hear of any dieners being fired because of alcoholism.

Another career contingency common to all of the dieners I have observed, interviewed, and heard about through other dieners and ex-dieners is the notorious status that becomes a part of the diener's identity. This point is most interesting, considering the pains the hospital goes through in separating clinical and anatomical pathology from the rest of the departments. Every morgue and autopsy room in every hospital I observed either had a separate building for these facilities or was located in the basement with the door reading "No admittance." Almost all hospital staff knew the locations of the morgue and autopsy room yet had never been there themselves. I have found that a permanent diener at a hospital becomes more recognizable to the staff and employees than the more renowned physicians. Sudnow also made reference to the fact that the diener was known throughout the hospital on this way to and from a death.

The diener has a unique position in pathology and medicine. When German pathologists first created the role over a hundred years ago, medicine was far from being the highly prestigious and status role it is today. Only in the last fifty to sixty years has the medical profession been able to lift itself to a position of controlling the healing arts and monopolizing the sub-universe of knowledge known as scientific medicine. In the beginning, the diener was trained by the pathologist to perform a complete gross autopsy (gross in the anatomical sense). This included the dissection of all organs including the brain plus the regular dienering work already described in the core activity section. The reasons for the change in the diener role in the last sixty years from "prosector" to "body preparer" are correlated quite closely with the intern and resident training programs emerging with the growth of hospitals. Because pathology has always been taught on a "learn one, do one, teach one" basis, the young physicians began to replace the diener, especially in teaching hospitals, and the duties of preparing the body before and after the prosection became the core activity. Since the diener had no professional role in medicine, he had to take the role pathology created. Since this new role has become the norm for the diener in medicine today, he finds himself working extremely close to a highly prestigious profession without reaping the benefits of prestige and money deserving of this relationship. After almost sixty years, this role has replaced the traditional German diener in the field of pathology and has created a problem for the pathologist in the process. Up to fifteen years ago, according to the pathologists interviewed for this study, the ratio of pathologists to clinicians was in a ratio beneficial to both areas of medicine. Since 1950-1955, pathologists have had difficulty in attracting medical students to the field. One of the fourth-year medical students interviewed told me he was the only student going into pathology out of a class of 150. When he told his advisor of his decision, the instructor "almost fell through the floor." A hospital in this study that was supposed to be a teaching situation for residents in pathology has failed to have one apply because there are no facilities for surgical pathology available. It appears that the trend in pathology, especially for residents and interns, is a move from gross autopsy to surgicals with the latter having the greater status. Because of this trend in resident programs, pathology has found itself confronted with a burdensome workload that keeps increasing each passing year. Logically, the diener should have been able to fill this breach by returning to the "traditional" role and assist with the gross pathology. However, this has not been the case. After sixty years in a role that has acquired no prestige and status, lower qualifications for entrance plus the stigma of working in a "morbid" occupation, the diener was in no position to reduce the burden on pathology. Since most dieners were only taught the "dienering" role, they were unable to return to the original level of competence once held. Pathology found itself in a dilemma. Should they retrain the dieners they now have and give them more money or should they create a new role within pathology thus hopefully eliminating the stigma associated with the term diener? At the present time, both ideas are being implemented, and the result of this movement in pathology will be taken up more explicitly in the next section.

As was pointed out in the introduction, there are four major classifications or diener types that are present in medicine today. The exact ratio of each of these roles is unknown except for the last one that will be described later. It is interesting to note a cyclical pattern present as each role has progressed through time, with the last type resembling the original role very closely.

Type I—The "Traditional" German Diener

This of course is the original diener role as created by the German pathologists. He was trained on the job by the physicians and was quite capable of completing a gross autopsy. His training in anatomy was very thorough, and his ability to dissect and detect pathology increased with experience and exposure within medicine. Being trained as a prosector takes years if one's training is dependent solely upon "on the job" contact with post mortems. Therefore, the "traditional" role of diener took someone dedicated to the field of medicine and has willingness to learn.

The "traditional" diener is still present in pathology today but in decreasing numbers, according to my observations. This type of diener is still highly valued by the physicians especially in the area of forensic pathology. The one "traditional" diener I have come across has been in the occupation since the age of seventeen, which has been a total of forty-three years "on the job" training; most of this time, he has been in forensic pathology at a large city hospital, which is associated with the medical examiners office within the county. The medical examiner I interviewed mentioned that he used to diener while going to medical school, and the "traditional" diener was his boss. Even though the medical examiner now has authority over the "traditional" diener, he is still treated by the diener as a medical student. Over the years, this "traditional" diener has become an expert in forensic pathology and is "involved in locating bullets and stab wounds in suicide or murder victims." Everyone in the entire hospital including the house staff has the greatest respect for this man and his role in pathology. As one doctor said, "He is worth his weight in gold." Most of the dieners at this particular hospital have stayed with the occupation for a number of years because the money is good, and they like the medical-legal work that can be very interesting at times.

The identity the "traditional" diener has with the hospital staff is quite consistent with his own role identity. However, outside the hospital community, he is still just a diener with all the connotations the name implies. This valuable member of the pathology team is viewed by outsiders the same way as the beginning diener and is looked upon as someone strange and morbid for being in such an occupation.

Type II—The "Modern" Diener

The "modern" diener emerged in medicine in the last fifty years as a result of the increase in resident programs in hospitals. Since the residents were found to be an extremely cheap source of labor for the hospitals, they were available to perform the gross autopsy "for the experience." The diener's role began to undergo changes during this period, and as a result, the core activity of prosector was reduced to the present core activity of skull removal and sewing the body.

It would appear that the "modern" diener is in the majority today, but this is not true. Another main criterion to be placed in the "modern" type is some degree of dedication to the occupation. This limits the number of dieners now working in the field to a small minority, for it is difficult to keep a qualified diener for any length because of the identity one has to assume when working in the role. Three such types were obtained for this study, but there are three additional ones working under the "traditional" diener previously mentioned that have not been interviewed. All "modern" dieners have worked in the field for fifteen to twenty-five years in the sample drawn for this study, but the exact numbers or ratio of the "modern" type is just not known. However, it appears that this diener type is definitely in the minority.

It would be most difficult to ask the dieners what type they would fit in, giving them only the above criteria. However, there is one career contingency that has proved to be quite helpful in the classification process. Most dieners can eviscerate the body when the pathologist or resident is pressed for time, but very seldom are they used as a prosector. This appears to be the one dividing criterion between the "traditional" and "modern" diener. One "modern" type has been asked to perform the autopsies for several physicians, and he has done so on many occasions, but he has never dissected the organs. He always saves them for the doctor in the refrigeration unit until he arrives to take samples for histology. The "traditional" diener has been trained by the pathologists to dissect the organs and take the samples while under supervision, even in a medical-legal case.

Type III—The "Transient" Diener

It is this third type of diener that is most abundant in pathology today. Since the status of the position is extremely low and has been so for the last sixty years, it is quite difficult to keep a diener in a permanent role situation.

This type of diener enters the occupation for reasons other than the pursuit and furtherance of medical science. Medical students utilize the role for money and the experience while attending school. There is no finer way of learning human anatomy. A few of the physicians interviewed were once dieners, and not all entered pathology.

Many of the "transient" type dieners use the position to make contacts with the funeral business. Most dieners meet the hearse drivers during a "pick up" and some are on a first-name basis with each other. Once a relationship is established, any job openings in a funeral home will be known, and the diener will be able to take advantage of it. One of the dieners interviewed has now been accepted to the mortuary school and will continue to diener while attending night classes. This particular diener did not use his role to break into the funeral business, but he was involved in forming an organization of dieners three years ago, composed of those who were all planning careers as morticians. At that time, there were nine such "transient" dieners either attending mortuary school or planning on such a course of action. The rationale behind the diener's organization was to place pressure on the various hospital administrations to increase the salaries of the position. Even though the organization never materialized, there have been salary increases for dieners in the last few years.

Another "transient" type is one who uses the position just to make some money while looking for a better job. The diener that I observed the longest was of this "transient" role and had problems working in other areas of the hospital because of the life style to which he was used to living. He had quit a paramedical position in a surgical unit prior to coming to the east coast because the head nurse did not like his long hair. As a diener, he was free to maintain his dress because of the low visibility of the role to other members of the hospital. Almost no one is concerned with the appearance of the diener since, as one hospital employee put it, "He would have to be a little crazy to be one in the first place."

Type IV—The Pathologists' Assistant

You may recall that pathology was in a dilemma when the workload increased and pathologists decreased during the last fifteen years. Many hospitals tried desperately to retain the qualified dieners and train them as "modern" or hopefully as "traditional" dieners, but as yet most pathology departments are still understaffed.

In the last five or six years, there has been a great deal of discussion in creating a paramedical role in anatomical pathology similar to the medical technicians now used in clinical pathology. The reasoning behind this planning was to relieve the pathologist, including the residents, from the routine tasks of a gross autopsy. It is interesting to note that this concern coincides with the salary increases that residents have begun to demand within medicine. Whatever the arguments may be, there has emerged in the last year the nucleus of a new paramedical career within pathology. I was quite hesitant to place this new career within the category of diener since one of the main objectives of the physicians who were behind the pathologists' assistant program was to remove the stigma associated with the diener role. However, viewing the entire trend, which has occurred in pathology in a sociological perspective, I am forced to see this new emerging role as the end of a cyclical pattern where the diener has moved from prosector to body preparer back again to prosector in the course of one hundred years. Not only has the title been changed, but also additional duties have been added to this new role, which if utilized by the profession of medicine will make it the invaluable role the diener once played in Germany. Since this new career cannot be analyzed in a page or two, the next section will deal with this most recent career in pathology.

Training of the Diener

The training of the diener within pathology has remained in its traditional role to some degree, for the doctor is usually responsible for training the diener. This varies from hospital to hospital, but generally, this is the case. Sometimes, the histologist or other nonphysician personnel are responsible for the diener's training, but very seldom. Many times the dieners are responsible for training the new man, especially if the new diener is working under a "traditional" or "modern" type.

It does not take too long to learn the core activity or the auxiliary ones in most cases. If a diener is seriously considering remaining in the role, he is constantly in a training period with the pathologists, for the knowledge of disease is constantly expanding and enlarging. As was pointed out previously, most dieners terminate their occupation in the early phases of the career since most do not see the role as a permanent one. Because there is such a turnover in this field, the training process is a continuing career contingency for the "traditional" or "modern" diener and a constant task of the pathologist. At one hospital, there has been one new diener every year for the last fifteen years, according to a histologist that has worked in the department that long.

All of the training is through observation of other dieners and the pathologists. During the training phase of the role, most of the real dirty work is given to the new diener, especially if a "traditional" or "modern" type is delegating the tasks. In a sense, the new diener becomes the older diener's assistant except in those cases where the diener is to assume all dienering responsibilities within a department.

One of the greatest assets in a pathology department is the quality of a trained and experienced diener. Once a diener leaves his role open, and the personnel department is unable to fill it due to shortage of people interested, it can create many problems for everyone. This occurred last year to one of the hospitals in the study. To rectify this situation, a medical student was trained to do "posts," but in the training period, many of the residents had to fill this void. Many times, the residents had to prepare the body, open and close the skull, eviscerate the body, and do all of the sewing, not to mention cleaning up afterward. Needless to say, this did not go over very well with the residents, and many fell behind on their cases because of it. This is only one example of what can happen when this role is vacated. I'm sure every hospital has experienced this at one time, especially in the last ten to fifteen years.

Personal Life of the Diener

What type of life does one lead that is constantly dealing with death? One of the most constant patterns in the career of the diener is the outside reaction to his identity. By outside, I mean those not connected with the pathology department or booking. Anyone walking in and out of the autopsy room is considered to be working with the dead bodies since no one else would walk into it. The stares one receives going in or coming out are quite noticeable. I recall during a "post" at one hospital, all the lights went out, and only the histologist and pathologists' assistant were present beside me. The pathologists' assistant was just about to go out the door and change the fuse when the histologist said he had better change it because if anyone would see the pathologists' assistant's bloody apron, someone would faint.

Sudnow observed in his study that the diener had a difficult time at the cafeteria since no one would eat lunch with him unless he was in a tie and white coat. My observations did not verify such treatment for the dieners and pathologists' assistant in this study. I did notice that one diener usually ate lunch with the stockroom clerk and his wife. The same diener was quite popular with the secretarial staff also and was considered a problem by some members of the pathology department because of his socializing with the hospital staff (females) during working hours.

When a resident or staff physician in pathology gives a party, the diener is left out. The pathologists' assistant has been invited to a few parties at doctor's houses but even he has his problems in this area. Most of the personal interactions concerned within this section will exclude the pathologists' assistant since a more complete summary in this area will be dealt with in the next section.

At the time of my observations at one hospital, the morgue was being expanded, and workmen were always present in the autopsy room for about three weeks. It was most interesting to view the faces of these men as they witnessed an autopsy procedure. A few of them would stand for minutes at a time and watch the diener and doctors remove the organs from the body. Not once did I see the workmen talk to each other during an autopsy and all the while maintaining an expressionless face. Outside the autopsy room, however, these workmen were quite friendly with the dieners. Every time the diener and I would pass these men in the hall during their lunch break, they would always ask the diener how everything was in the autopsy room, and the reply was always "pretty dead." This always produced a humorous response from the workmen, and they never failed to ask the diener the same question. Humor appears to be one of the major forms of interaction for the diener in his personal life. Every diener interviewed has acknowledged the fact that they are constantly being ribbed about their identity with their personal friends. Even the hospital staffs have asked the diener pertinent questions, which are designed to shock most people not working in this field. For example, a "modern" diener type told me he is always being approached by the hospital administrator and asked if he has any fresh livers for the cafeteria. Such forms of verbal interchange are a constant part of the diener's career, and everyone interviewed accepts it as a normal reaction to them. The medical examiner mentioned that one of the main qualifications of a diener is a sense of humor since "one cannot take a job like this very seriously without going crazy."[20] Some of the dieners mentioned that when they are asked what they do for a living, they just say, "I work for a hospital" and leave it at that. All the dieners agree that a sense of humor is vital for their occupation, and this is quite evident during an autopsy. Many times the dieners would tell the body to stay where it was and not move as they were leaving the room.

Most people are quite curious about the exact duties of the diener but are reluctant to inquire too far with questions. I recall at one of the parties I attended given by a diener for his personal friends (some nurses but no doctors were present) that one of the people wanted a complete description of his duties. The diener proceeded to pull out some pathology slides and show them around. He took great pains to show more graphic and more "interesting" slides in a pathological sense to those who were interested. Needless to say, he was able to elicit great facial and verbal expressions from his friends, and all agreed they could never work with dead bodies like the diener.

The dieners are always being confronted with questions concerning their occupation. This is definitely one career contingency that the diener experiences whether he is in training, or a "transient," "traditional," or pathologists' assistant.

Mistakes at Work

Since the diener has very little responsibility delegated to his role in pathology, any mistakes that he makes are usually not crucial and highly visible to the staff. There are a few points worth mentioning that should be included as mistakes.

Probably the most crucial mistake a diener can perform is cutting his hand while working on a hepatitis or TB "post." Once this occurs, his gloves are removed, the cut is washed with surgical soap, and the wound is then covered before re-gloving. After the "post" is completed, the diener then must get a tetanus shot to insure his safety. However, there is no guarantee that any of this preventive procedure will work, so dieners usually use two sets of gloves while working on an "active post."

The most common mistake that dieners are called for by the physicians includes severing organs during extraction. It is quite easy to slip with the saw when removing the skull and cut the brain or slip with the knife and open the bowel or gallbladder during evisceration. It is these last two mistakes that are more crucial than damaging the brain, for they can cause great olfactory distress to those in the autopsy room, which is an added burden to the pathologist and makes the dirty work dirtier.

One of the most damaging mistakes caused by a diener involved two medical-legal cases. According to the law, all forensic "posts" must be performed by a medical examiner since the diagnosis of death is crucial as to homicide or suicide. According to the medical examiner interviewed, there have been two incidences where the physician allowed the diener to do the prosection work on the "posts," and the dieners had to testify in court. Since that time, the dieners working with the medical examiner's office have been tightly restricted to just the core activity of the job except under close supervision. The "traditional" diener in this study does do prosection work for the medical examiner but only under supervision.

The Pathologists' Assistant

During the last twenty years in medicine, there has been a great deal of specialization involving every area and functioning of the human body. Much of the scientific advancement medicine has undergone has been due to this increase in the division of labor and the research that accompanies specialization. Pathology experienced this process when anatomical and clinical pathology were divided into separate entities with the option open to the physician to take one or both of the special boards if desired. When this specialization occurred in pathology, a number of paramedical positions were developed in order to assist the pathologist with the core activity of studying diseases. Most of the paramedical positions in pathology began settling around the clinical end of the field, and such roles as medical technologist, lab trainees, technicians, etc., were developed within medicine to perform the tests that the pathologist once did. In the anatomical field, new roles also developed because of specialization, and the role of histologist was created by medicine to aid with the preparation of microscopic slides—a task that was once the responsibility of the pathologist or the resident. During the last year, a new role has emerged in anatomical pathology that was designed to aid the pathologist in the autopsy procedure and train to write the final summary and interpretation of diagnosis as well. This new role resembles the one the "traditional" diener once held in many respects but has qualities that surpass the "traditional" diener in responsibility and status. It is this new role, this fourth diener type—the pathologists' assistant that shall be explored in the next few pages in relation to training, allocation of tasks, personal aspects, and a number of other variables that are a part of his work system.

Training the Pathologists' Assistant

As of this writing there are three pathologists' assistants working within medicine today. All three have been included in this study, but the main methodological procedure used for this study was observation of one of the pathologists' assistants at an urban hospital in New England. Two PAs were interviewed by telephone after completing the period of observation, and that information will be included in all aspects of the paramedical career.

All three pathologists' assistants have graduated from the program designed to train this new paramedical role by the Duke University medical school in Durham, North Carolina, in assistance with the Department of Veteran's Affairs in Washington, DC. All three men's past experiences are pertinent to the training of the PA since there were prerequisites to the program. The following are admission requirements of the pathology assistant training program manual as designed by medical personnel in the department of pathology at Duke.

Students with the following prerequisite qualify as candidates for the program:

1. High school graduate with a minimum of two years experience as a hospital corpsman or licensed practical nurse (LPN). Preference will be given to graduates of four-year accredited colleges and two-year accredited community college.
2. Completion of an application form
3. Three character references—preferably from a biology professor if applicable and two people who are not related to the individual.
4. All official high school transcripts or official college transcripts
5. Personal interview is encouraged when feasible.

The background of all three pathologists' assistants now working is quite varied. One of the PAs had completed four years of college and had taught high school before learning of the program at Duke. This man will be called Mr. A. Mr. A had first applied at Duke in relation to their physician assistant paramedical course and was informed of the new program by mail. Mr. B, the second pathologists' assistant interviewed, also learned about the program after applying for the physician's assistant program and was rejected for applying too late. Mr. B had some college training and was in the process of getting a BA in biology and chemistry at the time of the interview. Mr. C, the pathologists' assistant observed for three months for this study, had not attended college but was a medical corpsman in the US Navy for four years. Mr. C had also worked in various hospitals as surgical paramedical personnel before learning of the program from a doctor he had met in the Navy. All three men completed the twelve-month course at Duke, and the following is a description of the tasks as found in the introduction of the "Curriculum Guide and Training Manual for the Pathologists Assistant."

> The pathologists' assistant will assist the pathologist in the performance of autopsies even to the extent of performing portions of the autopsy under the direct supervision of the pathologist. The pathologists' assistant will collect all cultures, toxicological specimens, special specimens for studies, and any specimen deemed necessary for the pathologist. He will insure the orderliness of all records pertinent to the pathologist, arranging them in a manner expeditious for the personal use of the pathologist. The pathologists' assistant will maintain the photographic apparatus and take all gross pictures and

marked photomicrographs as directed by the pathologists. The pathologists' assistant will assume the responsibility of insuring that the pathologist's directions related to special histological techniques are carried out. In addition, he will supervise all subordinate personnel [the diener] directly related to the autopsy suite.[21]

In the training program, there are three main phases divided among two three-month sessions and one six-month phase, which includes both classroom and laboratory works. The first phase (three months) consisted of academic and didactic classroom work in the basic sciences and was used by the university as a screening device to eliminate those who were not able to grasp the basic concepts. The next three months deal with mandatory rotation in disciplines that are closely allied to pathology. One-month rotations were designed in each of the following areas: medical photography, microbiology, and histology. The remaining six months were spent on rotation with the pathology departments of Duke and Veteran's Administration Hospital, where the time was divided equally between "gross" and "microscopic" pathology. All work was done on an individual basis with supervision of department staff and third and fourth year residents. "In addition, students will participate in gross dissection, histological examination, processing and analyzing of morphologic, biochemical, and microbiological data, and the final interpretation and correlation of results."[22]

The exact academic curriculum for the entire course consisted of the following:

Course Lab	Total Hours	Lecture
Anatomy	96	4 hr/wk
Physiology	96	4 hr/wk
Histology	212	4 hr/wk
Bacteriology	212	4 hr/wk
Radiation safety	4	2 hr/wk
Radiological techniques	2	2 hr/wk
Pathology	240	6 hr/wk

Most of the classes were conducted exclusively for the pathologists' assistants, but they did attend some classes with medical technicians and, at one point, attended classes with first-year medical students in anatomy. A few times, medical students attended some of the PA courses on their own when they had time or were interested in a certain aspect of pathology. Mr. C mentioned that the medical interns and residents at Duke resented the program at first because the doctors felt the PA students could not possibly be qualified to perform postmortems with only the small amount of training given at Duke. However, the residents began to respect the new "position" even before the training period was completed. This change of attitude came about when there was a reduction of manpower in the pathology department, and the PAs were used to fill the gap.

Since the graduating of the three PAs last July 1970, there has been a change in the training aspects of the program. The most major change has been an increase in the overall course that now includes eighteen months of training with a possible further lengthening up to twenty-four months. I asked each of the PAs what changes in their training program they would like to see now that they've completed the course work and have had some experience in the field. All agreed that the program should be longer and have more practical work with the autopsy procedure. There were other interesting comments that reflect the identity of this new role and should be mentioned at this point. Both Mr. A and B would like to see the role of the PA extend into surgical pathology as well as autopsy. Since the core activity of surgical pathology deals with diagnoses, which are crucial for the surgeon and patient awaiting results, there can be no mistake in procedure. For this reason only, the third-year residents (sometimes second-year on a part-time basis) are allowed the status of performing surgicals. There appears to be a movement for residents in pathology from a strictly anatomical role the first year, to half surgical the second, to full surgical the third. It is important to keep in mind that as the resident moves closer to the surgical pathology role, his decisions become more important since he is working with a live patient. This nearness to the living seems to be one criterion of status for the pathology resident who usually deals only with dead bodies, and where most of his decisions are not crucial and restricted by time limits. There are some routine tasks even in surgical pathology called "scut work" or "minor surgical," which consist of cutting tonsils, prostate, skin, moles, warts, and amputations, which the PAs feel they should be allowed to perform. Since the resident gains status while moving toward the living, so should the pathologists' assistant.

Another suggestion made by the PAs was an increase exposure with medical students during the course work. One thought that the core course in pathology should be the same as that of the first-year medical students. It appears that the closer one gets to medical student curriculum, the more one can identify with the PA role. Since the training of the PA is designed to do the same tasks as the resident in pathology, it is no wonder that the PAs would want similar training.

Tasks and Work Setting

It is interesting to note that each of the three PAs have been utilized by pathology in slightly different but important ways. Each work setting has created different tasks and, in turn, has created different roles for each of the three PAs. From the previous discussion, the reader has some idea of what the PA was exposed to and a vague notion of what would be expected of such a person within a pathology department. Since the role is so new to medicine, most pathologists have a difficult time in determining how to use the PA. A more complete discussion of this will appear in the next section. However, for the most part, each PA was concerned with how a department would utilize his training before committing himself for a position. Even though there was no guarantee, each PA had some idea how he would be used before moving from Duke. Since each PA has performed differently in the year, I will describe the tasks and work setting of each and then make some generalizations at the end.

Mr. A seems to be an appropriate beginning not only alphabetically but also in movement from Duke. Mr. A remains at Duke after his training and has been utilized almost entirely in a teaching role. Not only does he instruct the PAs in training, but he is also responsible for teaching first-year residents and interns in the procedures of gross anatomical pathology. He has been teaching since July 1970, and most of his time is consumed in this way. One of the main reasons for staying at Duke was to get more training while teaching. However, unless the residents are really busy, Mr. A does not have the opportunity to do "posts," and getting more experience has been difficult. At the present time, Mr. A is working with ten residents plus medical students. Since there are 650 "posts" each year at the hospital, plus 250 more at the Veteran's Administration Hospital, the department can get extremely busy at times, which permits him to do some "posts" during each month. Mr.

A is not in charge of the one diener and two embalmers who work in the department, but he definitely has a higher status role than either one. Most of the training he has received has been utilized except for the photography since Duke has their own photographer. For the most part, Mr. A is utilized like a resident, for he is allowed to do a "complete" autopsy. By complete, I mean beginning with the evisceration of the body, dissection of organs, gross autopsy summary, clinical summary, microscopic summary, postmortem bacteriology or chemical summary, plus a final analysis of all of the above, which is called a final summary and interpretation. Many times, this also includes a review of the literature that requires more time. Since the pathologist is the only one allowed to indicate the cause of death, the final summary and interpretation must be signed out with a staff member. This applies to the residents also, who are on "rotation" with the department. This entire procedure can take sixteen to twenty hours and, many times, even longer.[23] Since the body cannot lie around in the morgue until final summary and interpretation is completed (which can take three to four weeks in a majority of the cases), the "preliminary anatomical diagnosis" (PAD) is used for death certificate purposes. The PAD is written after gross autopsy, and Mr. A has his diagnosis approved by senior staff during the "gross conference" within the department.

The work schedule for Mr. A runs from 8:00 a.m. to 4:30 p.m. with no calls on weekends. Mr. A has never had to do the diener work all the time he has worked as a PA, and he has no problems with the residents. All three of the PAs reported some problems with the older residents when the program first began, so Mr. A's statement is important.

Although Mr. A does not perform too many "posts," he did begin his first at the end of July of 1970 and was responsible for all of the procedure from PAD to final summary and interpretation. All of this indicates that the PA role in this work system is moving in the direction of resident status, which is a far cry from the status of the "traditional" diener once held in Germany, and now holds within pathology today. In the process, the resident's status is changed by the introduction of this new role, for more time is now available for "surgicals." Even though this is not too evident in Mr. A's work setting, the other two work systems where the PA has been introduced certainly show this movement of the residents. This substantiates Hughes's cleanliness-uncleanliness continuum, which he has found to exist within medicine, and the status that accompanies each.

Mr. B's work setting has developed on somewhat different lines. Mr. B was hired exclusively to do "posts." He began his first "post" two weeks after he arrived in July of last year (1970). His first "post" was complete from PAD to final summary and interpretation. At the time of the interview, there was only one resident in anatomical pathology doing "posts" because the department was undergoing administrative change. This lack of residents has increased the status of the PA role at Mr. B's hospital. There are four to five residents on rotation in the department but only one on surgicals. However, these "surgical path" residents do share the weekend calls for "posts," so Mr. B is on weekend call every fourth week. There are three dieners working with the department, two of which are in training. The one that has been at the hospital since 1964 is called the supervisor diener, and from his job description, it sounds like a "modern" type. Mr. B is in charge of the dieners actions, for if anything is dirty in the autopsy room, the staff tells Mr. B to tell the dieners. Mr. B's sign-out procedure is different from Mr. A's, for he signs out directly with a staff member with no clearance with the chief resident. Many times, the microscopic and final summary and interpretation are combined, but there is always a sign-out after gross with the staff either in conference or on a one-to-one basis. Mr. B does on the average about three "posts" per week, and so far this year, he has completed 53 percent of all the cases in the department. Again, we see the same pattern emerging in Mr. B's work setting, where his duties and responsibilities are similar to a resident even more so as compared with the other pathologists' assistants. In almost every respect, Mr. B is treated like a resident. He has done everything he was trained to do except photography since the hospital has their own. Since he has done over half of the "posts," he usually gets the interesting cases as well. So far, he has completed three "reportable" cases, and his name will appear on the research articles if they are published. This is another indicator of Mr. B's status location as a PA within his department.

In most cases, Mr. B does not handle the dienering work, but he has done some of the diener's tasks on some restricted cases. Since Mr. B has been with the department, he has reorganized the entire autopsy room and has begun a file of the old organs that are kept for the interns and residents as study aids. One of the problems Mr. B has confronted is the amount of work that he has experienced since his arrival. Because he is responsible for three complete "posts" a week, he is always behind in his work reports or the final summary and interpretations and has little time to complete his microscopic work. After completing his BA degree in biology and chemistry, he plans to go for either a PhD or MD degree while still continuing in the PA role. Again we see a PA functioning in a resident capacity with all of the responsibility that accompanies that role. We see a PA looking toward higher credentials that may eliminate him from his present PA role if he should reach them. It will be interesting to see the career contingencies that arise within this role in the next ten to twenty years if most PAs elect to continue their education beyond the core course from which they emerged.

The work setting of Mr. C is completely different from the above two. For one thing, he was not allowed to do a "post" for almost four months after his arrival at the hospital and then only under supervision. During these four months, most of Mr. C's tasks were those of a diener, and the role of the transient diener that was with the department fell to the level of janitor. From November to January, Mr. C was permitted one "post" a week but was not included on a full rotation basis. Many times, Mr. C didn't even get a chance to do one a week, and most of his energy and training was directed toward other tasks besides the core activity as defined by the training program. During the period of observation from January to April, Mr. C was just beginning to do some of the core activities, but at no time was he considered doing resident tasks. He never did one complete autopsy during the time preceding my observation nor during the three months I studied the department. Just before I left, he was in the process of writing up a final summary and interpretation for one of the doctors (one that was at Duke with Mr. C), but he felt that since he had not utilized his knowledge to his fullest potential, he had found this task somewhat more difficult than at Duke. One of the areas that Mr. C was most useful in applying his training is the area of photography. Up to his arrival, the residents were forced to take the pictures of the organs, and since they were not trained, many of the pictures were lost. Mr. C was most instrumental in organizing the surgical room as well as the autopsy suite and was responsible for setting up the organs for the "gross conference" and the brains for the brain-cutting conference, both of which were held once a week. Mr. C was also responsible for organizing the slides for the slide conference for the residents and staff within the department. Even though Mr. C was not allowed a complete "post," he did write up the PAD and the clinical summary that involves the complete hospital and medical history of the patient prior to death. Many times, it was the clinical summary that occupied many hours of Mr. C's core activity when he was allowed access to this area. Mr. C was also writing up the microscopic summary during the first half of my observation period but was later relieved of this task by the head of anatomical pathology. It seemed that a medical student was in need of a microscope, so the department head walked into Mr. C's office and told him he could not allow him to read the microscopics since Mr. C would have to have them checked again anyway during sign-out, which requires too much time of the staff. At this point, the microscope went out the door, and the PA's status was reduced somewhat from its previous state that was precarious to begin with. A complete evaluation of the social psychological processes that evolved during Mr. C's emergent role period as a PA will be dealt with more extensively in the next section. At this point, it is only necessary to demonstrate the restricted work system Mr. C was subjected to as compared to the other PAs in the field. The only task, which Mr. C was allowed to perform in regard to his training, was the photography work and the organization of photographic slides into disease categories. Most of the other core activities were limited by the department that was the major source of conflict not only for the PA and his role identity formation but for the department staff as well.

Personal Aspect of the PA Role

Since one's identity is so closely aligned with one's occupation, it is interesting to see how the personal life of a pathologists' assistant is affected by his identity with pathology. Many times, one's occupational status can be measured by the personal interaction of the individuals during and after working hours. Who invites whom to a party? What is the process of introductions that are instituted within the department and when new members arrive? Both of these are good indicators of where one fits into the occupational structure of an organization. Another important identity process that every occupational role must confront is telling of one's place in the work system to strangers either at social gatherings or within the organizational structure itself.

The formation of the PA role first began with the training program at Duke. During the twelve-month training period, there was an average of one party a week, and most of these were attended by not only the pathologists' assistants but medical technologists, residents, and interns as well. It is interesting to note that the dieners were not invited to these functions even though they had been with the department for some time. Even when they were invited, they did not attend. Once in awhile, the staff would invite only certain occupational and professional groups such as the medical technologists, pathologists' assistants, and residents all at different times, so there was some segregation involved but very little. Most of these functions were mixed with no indication that status movement was an important aspect of the training process.

In relation to social functions at the individual work settings of each PA, there were some interesting processes emerging in their personal lives that are important to mention. For the most part, all of the PAs have been invited to staff parties at each hospital. In two of the cases, the dieners were also invited expect when policy was being discussed at Mr. B's work setting, and then only the staff, residents, and PA were invited. However, there have been some social functions where Mr. C was excluded and the secretary of the department told him it was an oversight on one occasion.

When the social functions the PAs attended were not connected with the hospital, there were some common patterns of response that nonmedical people make toward the role of PA. Many times, it is the same response that dieners received. For Mr. A, the general reaction toward his role was disgust if the person was not familiar with medicine. When explaining that his core activity deal with autopsies, there were usually facial expressions demonstrating negative connotations toward the role. Mr. B said that this was also the common response, but he emphasized that women were more apt to indicate horror and revulsion than men. Mr. C indicated that there are three questions everyone asks when inquiring about his occupational status, which becomes a part of the verbal interchange at a party. They are the following: (1) What do you do; (2) What is a pathologist; and (3) Where do you fit into the picture? After Mr. C's explanation concerning his job, all lay people make a comment as to how they could never do such a line of work, i.e., working with dead bodies. All the PAs have indicated that only those familiar with the medical field give an interest to their role in pathology.

The lunch and coffee breaks I observed in Mr. C's work setting are quite interesting. Most of the time, I had coffee with the diener and his friend, the stockroom employee. In every case, the PA would either eat lunch with his wife, who was a secretary in the surgical department, or eat alone. Doctors ate with doctors, nurses with nurses, and nurse's aides with nurse's aides, orderlies with orderlies, and secretaries with secretaries. There were some exceptions to this rule but very few. Since the role definitions are quite rigid within medicine, the fact that the PA had little choice in his companions at breaks is not surprising.

Another example of Mr. C's status in relation to where he stands in the department hierarchy on a personal interaction basis was the procedures of introducing the new personnel to the staff. In every case, Mr. C was not formally introduced by the anatomical department head or the chief resident to any of the arriving members, and Mr. C ended up having to introduce himself to the new residents or medical students. During this introduction, Mr. C would also have to include an explanation of his exact duties within the department, since most people had never heard of a PA before.

Emergence of the PA Role in Medicine

Because the role of PA has only been introduced in the last year, it is difficult to formalize any generalizations concerning where the career of the pathologists' assistant will eventually reside within pathology, but there are some common patterns, which have become apparent even at this stage of emergence of the new role.

One of the most interesting processes I call is the "pair-group emergence procedure," which two of the PAs have been involved in during their introduction to medicine. It was a major concern of the Duke training staff that the pathologists' assistant be situated in a work system where the tasks and training were known to at least one of the members within the department of pathology. In order for this to occur, each of the PAs had to move with one of the staff physicians so as to insure that the training would be utilized to its fullest extent. Since Mr. A remained at Duke, this "pair group" only concerned those that were interested in moving away from the school. Mr. B accompanied a physician that was to assume a department head in pathology at the hospital. Whether there is any correlation between the status of Mr. B as a resident and the fact that the department chairman was once in the Duke PA training program remains to be seen, but it appears that the "pair-group" is most instrumental in the emergence procedure of this new role. This same "pair-group" was found with Mr. C, but the physician with whom he moved was not in a position of power to influence the already-existent power structure within the department, which might be an explanation of Mr. C's relative status deprivation as measured by the other two PAs. It appears that Mr. B's status position has been set as the ideal by the other PAs, for both of them are seriously considering moving to Mr. B's hospital work setting in hopes of obtaining the position and responsibilities for which they were trained, i.e., a complete autopsy procedure. Had Mr. A moved, he would have certainly been a part of a "pair-group," but in many ways, he was also part of this process since his role was known to those in the department at Duke, and his status was quite similar to a resident in most cases.

Even though the "pair-group" process was initiated by Duke to insure that pathologists' assistants would be guaranteed a place in pathology, there was another indicator that even this will not be totally successful. It was quite apparent that the PA's status is determined by the department and work system within which he worked. The more power the physician in the "pair-group" had within the department, the more status accorded to the role of PA. However, in those departments, where the "pair-group" had little or no influence upon decision making in regard to PA status, it was quite possible in the next few years that each department will be able to shape the role of PA to its own liking. This process was more apparent in Mr. C's case, for many of his tasks for which he was trained were simply not utilized by the pathology department, and the role became quite rigid in regard to restrictions of procedures dealing with the autopsy. At the time of observation, Mr. C was being utilized by his department the same way the "traditional" diener was used in Germany, i.e., completing just the gross autopsy and dealing only with his first step in a complete autopsy procedure.

During the course of the observation with Mr. C, the head of clinical and anatomical pathology was interviewed to determine exactly where the role of the PA should be within pathology. His answer was quite straightforward, and he, in essence, stated that the role of the PA should be what it is already within the department. That included taking care of the autopsy room, performing gross autopsy under supervision, identifying the slides, doing the photography, and knowing something of the staining procedure. When asked if the department would hire another PA if Mr. C should leave, the chief pathologist replied that they were planning on hiring another PA even if the present one remained. He then went on to outline a plan to train his own PAs in conjunction with a local university's medical technology school. If such a program did develop out of Mr. C's department, it would be most certain that there would be little resemblance with Duke's curriculum, and most PAs would become instant "traditional" dieners. If this process continued to expand, it would resemble the process that is common with the different schools of nursing, which have devised so many varied programs that it is difficult to determine qualified people, and the role of pathologists' assistant will have an identity crisis to undergo for many years to come. Even with the "pair-group" bond, there is no guarantee that the PA will make a successful role emergence into medicine, but with the advent of varied schools springing up, shaping their own brand of PA, there is little hope of maintaining continuity within this new career's training program and role identity in pathology.

Divesting Process as a Career Contingency

As the role of the diener has moved to its original position in medicine, it is quite apparent that the identity associated with the role has also changed. It is quite apparent in medicine today that training of the diener from "body preparer" to prosector is just not feasible for pathology since the costs involved to train such a person just to have him regarded as "just another diener" will not work. The emergence of the "transient" diener is proof of what can happen when status and responsibility are low in regard to this position in pathology. It has become apparent to medicine that in order to relieve this manpower shortage, the entire identity of the role must change along with the duties. This, of course, is what has been the rationale behind the PA program and is based upon the change of symbolic manipulation common in attitudinal theories.[24] This "divesting process" within the diener career is culminated with the emergence of the pathologists' assistant that may be helpful in reducing some of the stigma associated with the occupation. If the PA can maintain a close identity with resident status and become a part of the "clean" occupations within medicine by becoming a part of the surgical pathology procedure, this "divesting process" may be the most important career contingency facing the role of the PA in the coming years. There are many process levels involved in this career contingency that should be kept in mind before continuing to the next section. Not only are structural elements such as roles, departmental hierarchy, and values included in this "divesting process" of the diener-pathologists' assistant, but social psychological functions within medicine itself are being reoriented.

Social Psychological Relationships Involved in an Emergent Divesting Process Role in Medicine

> The proper study of the division of labor will include a look at any system of work from the points of view of all kinds of people involved in it, whether their position is high or low, whether they are at the center or near the periphery of the system.[25]

Such a statement includes the social psychological processes that are involved in all social interaction. Since we are dealing with the profession of medicine, it becomes necessary to distinguish certain roles that have been delegated downward and the expectations one has of these particular roles, when working in and with the role. As was pointed out earlier, it is quite apparent the amount of power the physician has in regulating paramedical careers, while working within the medical culture. When one begins to investigate this controlling process, it becomes necessary to view the interaction that ensues not only from the control or medical side but from the controlled or paramedical side as well. Since the medical culture is strongly dependent upon the sick seeking out the physician, much of the medical culture is involved with coordinating this division of labor at the hospital level. The reliance of medicine upon various procedures of bureaucratic processes is no secret to anyone who has had an encounter with a hospital. The exact power positions within this bureaucracy is always maintained by the medical profession with all roles, status, task assignments, control mechanisms, and goals within the medical culture being defined and influenced by the doctors.

This study, and this chapter in particular, is concerned with the effect medicine has on this new emergent divesting process role and vice versa. Up to this point, we have seen how the PA role has been introduced into the medical bureaucracy through the pair-group process, a brief view of the problems, and conflicts that have been confronted by the different workers within pathology because of this new role. We have also seen the divesting process that is a part of this new career and some of the effects this has produced upon the diener's role. There has also been some reference to role conflicts within the pathology department where this PA role has been introduced, but up to this point, there has been no framework presented from which to analyze all of these interactions. It is the purpose of this section to introduce some theoretical perspective from which to give meaning to the interactions that have taken place between the PA and the others in the work system.

Role Theory and Bureaucratic Medicine

Since we are primarily concerned with a paramedical role, an emergent role so to speak, there must be some clear understanding of what is meant by the term *role*. So far, role has been used rather loosely in this study and especially when discussing the role of medicine within society. However, before proceeding any further, it has become necessary to be much more explicit with the term. There are a number of definitions that utilize the term *role,* depending upon the social and cultural context in which it is used. As was already pointed out, the medical profession is forced to delegate tasks and responsibility within a hospital, in the best bureaucratic tradition, in order to maintain uniformity and order within the division of labor. Because of this reliance upon bureaucratic organization within the medical culture, the term *role* has played a large part in the delegating of tasks, just as in other bureaucratic settings. The term *role* is usually looked upon as a position that can influence behavior within social interaction tradition and the equating of role with overt behavior in the anthropological sense.

Gouldner makes a distinction between manifest and latent roles. He maintains that a role can be performed differently, depending upon how the role is defined by the role taker.[26] J. Milton Yinger qualifies Goulder's definition even further by dividing latent into active and passive, where the latter is used to mean that one which has learned but not now utilized in action. Yinger has further distinguished latent as an active role but inappropriate to use at the same time as the manifest role.[27] At this point, we can see that there are a number of distinctions that must be kept in mind when using the term *role.* Generally, there tends to be some degree of consensus about which tasks would be performed by which people within an organization; that is, expectations begin to become stabilized, and the emergence of norms begins to cluster around task processes. It is at this point that roles begin to form and behavior becomes influenced by the normative order. This role process is quite common in a bureaucratic structure, for norms are usually implemented on the basis of task performance and needs of the organization, disregarding the personality of the individual who is placed into the role.

This is especially true for those working in a medical bureaucracy, for most of the roles are quite rigidly assigned and performed on the orders of medical science and those who represent this esoteric body, namely the doctors. What happens, however, when a new role is introduced into this medical culture and normative expectations must arise out of the social interaction within the system? This is the question that this section will hope to answer, in part, when the role of PAs observed in a new social setting, which has never encountered such a role previously.

Since there are no clear-cut role expectations on the part of staff and residents toward the pathologists' assistant, one can expect some conflicts to emerge at different points between the PA and the other medical roles, working in pathology. The exact location of these conflict points will not be indicated for a few more pages, but it is important to keep in mind that these conflicts influence not only the PA's identity but the other medical roles as well. For example, if a PA is trained to perform the complete autopsy procedure and do the same tasks of the resident, what happens to the role of the resident in the autopsy suite? If the residents begin to expect certain role behavior from the PA and this expectation is different from that of the staff, what becomes of the first behavioral set and what changes in their identities do the residents undergo when their expectations are not realized by the PA? How are the identities of the staff members altered by the emergence of the PA role within their department? What type of control mechanisms and leadership roles will be utilized by the staff to (1) establish parameters about the role of the PA, (2) utilize this new role effectively while still maintaining control, (3) delegate more or less responsibility depending upon the work setting, and (4) determine how to treat this new role within the bureaucratic structure and outside the department on a personal basis? Different members of the pathology department have asked all of these questions since the introduction of the PA role. Even after the observation period, many questions had remained unanswered for many members of the department, but it was quite apparent that the PA role had developed quite definite behavioral expectations for the department members during the three months this researcher was present.

For the analysis of this data, found between the interaction of the PA with other medical workers, I have relied primarily upon Thibaut and Kelley's work, *The Social Psychology of Groups,* which is the most comprehensive work produced to date on interpersonal relations and group functioning. There are a number of other social psychological sources used for this study, but they will be mentioned in the body. It is important to keep in mind that much of the theoretical perspective in the next few pages will be grounded in Thibaut and Kelley's work, and I will borrow heavily, not only in theory but in terminology as well.

The Work System of the PA

This entire section deals exclusively with the interactions observed during the three months this researcher was present in the pathology department, where the PA had been introduced six months previously. The PA arrived at New England Urban Hospital at the end of July 1970, after completing the PA training program. At the beginning of this introduction of the PA to this particular hospital, there were no normative expectations surrounding this new role, and this was quite evident during the early stages of the emergent process. So far, I have been able to identify four stages in this emergent process that have taken place in Mr. C's work setting. Stage 1 may occur prior to any contact with this new role, or it may begin with the first social interaction during the interview. It became apparent that some members of the department had heard of some "talk" of this new role and had developed some expectations concerning the PA's exact duties. For these people, stage 1 began prior to contact, for they were aware of its emergence. For those that had heard of the role during the initial contact of the interview, they had only two months to contemplate how the role should be used within the department. Stage 2 is called the "preemergence" period and concerns that point in the interaction where the new role meets the staff and gets to "know his way around." In some ways, this stage is quite similar to Caplow's ritual of initiation. For the PA, this means being in a subordinate position to medicine to begin with, must accept those tasks as assigned to him from the staff and in a way is initiated into the medical culture. The third stage of the emergent role process I call the "high role flexibility" period, and it is a Yinger term, which means there are present many permissive norms available to the role player.[28] Even though there are no clear-cut norms formed in the emergent process at stage 3, there is a considerable degree of flexibility due to the lack of any stringent normative expectations surrounding the role. In many ways, this third stage is a "feeling out" period for the medical culture, testing the abilities prior to the relinquishing of responsibility to this subordinate position. Stage 4, the "partial role emergence" period, is the time when this new role begins to establish some form of identity within the medical culture, and norms are formed to solidify the role.

Each stage, which the PA has passed through in this emergent process within the pathology department, has shaped his identity and role tasks and affected the interpersonal relations between him and the other department members. The last section will illustrate the effect each stage has upon the PA and group functioning in general.

One of the major factors in the emergent role process is, of course, the conflicts that center on the PA role. Yinger has divided role conflicts into internal and external conflicts, and this distinction is necessary for our purposes. Internal role conflict includes that interaction that occurs when a role player has internalized a role that includes contradictory behavior patterns of "when he occupies two or more positions that carry incompatible role expectations."[29] These incompatibilities may or may not be perceived also. External role conflict occurs when an individual is confronted with inconsistent behavior expectations from two or more members in the group or organization. This too may not be perceived. The PA has confronted both of these types of role conflict, and a complete discussion of this will appear in the last section.

There are other role conflict distinctions that Gross, Mason, and McEachern make that are also pertinent to this study. "An individual is confronted with an intrarole conflict if he perceives that others hold different expectations for him as the incumbent of a single position . . . In intrarole conflict, an individual perceives that others hold different expectations for him as the incumbent of two or more positions."[30] These conflict roles will also be utilized in this report as well as those dealing with role conflict resolution, which will be introduced when the emergent role process begins to evolve into stage 5. This again will take place in the last section of this chapter when some of the role conflicts begin to be recognized by the PA, staff, and residents.

Status, Tasks, and Power in Emergent Role Formulation

One theoretical position that Thibaut and Kelley utilize throughout their work deals with exchange theory and its application to interpersonal relationships. From this, Thibaut and Kelley formulated a reward and cost decision-making procedure that they call the comparison level (CL). CL is a standard by which the person evaluates the rewards and costs of a given relationship in terms of what he feels he should get from the interaction. Those relationships that fall above the CL would be "satisfying" to the individual in most cases, and those outcomes that fall below CL would be relatively "unsatisfying" and unattractive. The comparison level alternative (CL alt) can be defined as the lowest level of outcomes a member will accept in regard to the available alternative opportunities. As soon as the outcomes of the relationship drop below CL alt, the member will leave the relationship. Peter Blau has a similar concept in his work,[31] which he calls "comparative expectations." This refers to expectations of profits or rewards minus the costs. For a relationship to continue, it does not depend entirely upon the rewards one receives but the ratio between the rewards and costs. As people become accustomed to a certain level of satisfaction with a relationship, they begin to take it for granted and expect at least that particular level of gratification to remain stable in the future.

Since the interaction between the PA and other workers in pathology is taking place within the bureaucratic medical culture, the intrinsic aspects of the relationship are not crucial since most interaction is measured by role behavior that is most certainly extrinsic according to Blau. In actuality, one can associate with another person for both kinds of social rewards, but the intrinsic attractiveness of a person is difficult to identify and measure in a limited study of this nature. This researcher has found that much of the interaction in pathology is grounded in role behavior. What are the benefits one can add to the pathology team to accomplish the common goal of final summary and interpretation? In many respects, this interaction resembles Winch's theory of complimentary needs.[32] This states that one member can do something for the other at low cost and yet provide the partner with high rewards. This means that each person can do something for the other one that that person cannot do for or by himself.

It is interesting to note that the training program outlined the rewards and costs of becoming a pathologists' assistant during the very first interview with the candidates. All three of the men were told that they would have an extremely hard time of breaking into the medical culture since it was such a new role. This preparation helped to formulate a CL for the men before they even began their training. We will see very shortly how Mr. C's CL has shifted from its initial "don't expect too much" stage to its present level.

Status of Each Occupation in the PA's Work Setting

Upon Mr. C's arrival to the pathology department at New England Urban Hospital, there were a number of status systems already formed, which consisted of the staff physicians first—and second-year residents, medical students at various stages of study, and varying degrees of paramedical roles, which ranged from histologists, medical secretaries, histology technicians, and diener. During the time of this researcher's observation, it appeared there was consensus concerning the status of most every position or role in the work setting with the exception of the PA. The doctor or the staff held the high-status positions with the head resident, second-year residents, first-year residents, fourth-year medical students, and remaining medical students, each occupying status positions below the doctors in the order presented. One can readily see that the medical profession dominates the stratified status system in the pathology department. The remaining work roles fall below those directly engaged with the medical profession. This was the only status position Mr. C was aware of when joining the department, and this was the status the staff also established for the PA since he was looked upon as occupying a role similar to a laboratory technician. As compared to the other PAs, Mr. C's status is visibly lower but would occupy a middle-status position within the department itself. The lower-status position in Mr. C's department would include the histology technicians and the diener and perhaps the medical secretaries as well. During the four stages of role emergence that the PA has passed through at New England Urban Hospital, he was constantly aware of the status the other PAs had reached at the other hospitals, and he used them to establish new CLs for himself. Since the other two PAs had obtained some status position quite similar, if not the same as the residents, Mr. C was constantly trying to move toward resident status himself. The result of this movement has been the source of role conflict within the department, and the results of this conflict will be described at the end of this section.

One of the key indicators of one's status within a work system is the type of tasks one performs. In a way, the physician is delegating a portion of his responsibility to other roles and since the tasks within pathology are set by the doctors, they have a great deal of power to determine all of the status positions and almost all of the outcomes within the interaction. When Mr. C first arrived (stage 2) in the department, the tasks he was assigned were quite similar to those performed by the transient diener. Such a status position for a PA would certainly fall below his CL, had it not been for the fact that Mr. C's CL was already set fairly low by the training school to begin with. The fact still remains that Mr. C's tasks and status were most definitely set by the physicians in power. Thibaut and Kelley's theory suggests "that the person with high power will be able to enjoy more frequently the best reward-cost positions available . . . Having more to offer (or to threaten to withdraw), he is better able to induce the low-power person to perform such behavior as he, the high-power person, desires rather than vice-versa."[33] Thibaut and Kelley make a further distinction in the use of power within a relationship. "If by varying his behavior, A can affect B's outcomes regardless of what B does, A has fate control over B . . . A second kind of power is called behavior control. If by varying his behavior, A can make it desirable for B to vary his behavior too then A has behavior control over B."[34] In this respect, we see that the medical profession most definitely has fate control over all emerging paramedical roles in general and the pathologists' assistant in particular.

Social Interaction within the Department

Now that some theoretical background has been established to evaluate the various behavior observed by this researcher between the emergent PA role and the remaining work system, it will be much easier to see where this new role has been placed.

One of the major points of interaction for Mr. C was between himself and the diener. When Mr. C first arrived, he was given the "diener work," which left the diener's role ill defined. Mr. C did the dienering work from August to November when he was finally allowed to perform the prosector's duties. Even during my observations in January, February,

March, and April, it appeared there was some strain between the PA and the diener because of the role conflicts. As a result of this conflict, the diener was reduced to a janitor's position and remained so throughout this study. This lack of role consensus on the part of the diener increased his socializing on the job that he was criticized for by the staff. Yinger points out that Merton discusses a number of ways by which a person may seek to reduce the difficulties in performing his role, which should be mentioned here.[35] The fact that all role activities are observable to all in the work setting is one way to escape from the conflict. New England Urban Hospital was responsible for the pathology work at another nearby hospital, and many times, the diener would use this time to escape from the work setting and take his time in returning. Prior to the arrival of the PA, the histologist was responsible for the diener, but the PA was delegated this task by the staff. This seemed to increase the conflicts between the PA and diener since they were both competing for the same tasks in the work setting. The PA reprimanded the diener in front of two residents in the surgical cutting room for not cleaning the autopsy room, and from that point on, the diener and PA were on conflicting terms. The diener was certainly the low-status position within the department, and much of his behavior resembled that described by Merton above. Kelley and Cohen found that persons in low-status, undesirable positions were found to initiate a large amount of irrelevant information during working hours, which was used as an escape or diversion from the dirty work of the position.[36] This was certainly true of the diener in this particular work setting, for he would constantly talk of everything to everyone and had the reputation of "talking your leg off." There was one task for which the diener derived some status even from the staff, for he was able to remove the brain and spinal cord together without damage to either, which was a constant source of amazement to one of the physicians. I believe it was this one status task that kept the diener at New England Urban Hospital since most every other duty was devoid of any recognition. After Mr. C began to perform the prosector work, the diener again became the diener role in the department, but there was still conflict between him and the PA.

One of the more interesting role conflicts for the PA was with the residents within the department. Mr. C was trained to perform a complete autopsy and internalized such a role during his one year of training. After working at New England Urban Hospital, this manifest internalized role became latent and, in Yinger's terms, a passive role as well. No longer did Mr. C have the semi-resident status he once held during his training period. Mr. C told every resident upon his arrival that he was capable of performing the prosector's tasks and thought he should be allowed to do so in the department. It is most interesting to note that the residents called a meeting with the staff in November (four months after the PA arrived) and demanded that Mr. C be allowed to be on rotation with the residents because of the heavy workload. It was at this point that the PA began to do posts on a somewhat regular basis in the department. Besides this incident, there was further indication that the PA was moving from his initial transient diener role to resident status. Several times during the observation period, complaints were verbalized by some of the residents to Mr. C about the behavior of one of the residents, and Mr. C would discuss it with them. Each wanted the other to tell the problem resident to curtail his specific objectionable qualities. In essence, it would appear that some of the residents began to view the PA role as a peer in several respects even though the staff felt differently about it. This differential treatment from the staff and residents brought about external conflict to the PA role, and Mr. C was confronted with inconsistent behavior from about three to four members of the department. I recall one point that illustrates that the PA role was emerging to resident peer status. During a slide preparation by Mr. C, there was a question concerning the effect of a brain tumor upon the motor activities of the person who had it. The PA asked a resident what the effect would be, and he gave him his opinion. He later returned after consulting with the doctor who had the patient history and explained that the tumor had caused no symptoms to the patient. This extra information and effort on the part of the resident seemed to surprise the PA and diener, for they did not expect any reply whatsoever. Mr. C was always on a friendly basis with the residents, and the residents believed Mr. C was an asset to the department. The fourth-year medical student believed the PA to be well-qualified for the prosector role but felt that some of the explanations Mr. C gave during the conferences were from memory instead of through actual understanding. He added that the PA knew more anatomy than most of the residents and doctors. When asked what he thought the role of the PA should be, he stated that the PA should be available to assist the residents. "When there is a tight squeeze, he is capable of being a resident." Such a statement certainly indicates that the PA role in this department has reached a status somewhere between a medical student and resident, which is certainly more than it was when he first arrived. One of the second-year residents felt that "the PA should not be considered a resident but should be available to fill the void in anatomical pathology." Another resident felt that in a teaching situation that exists at New England Urban Hospital, the PA should not take a prominent role, but in a private hospital, where the workload is very heavy and there are no residents, the PA should have complete responsibility, including final summary and interpretation. Almost all of the residents felt there would be a period of waiting on the part of the PA because of the role pathology plays in the medical culture. Since pathology is utilized as a service by the clinician, much of the problems the PA role will face in its acceptance will depend upon the clinician's attitudes toward this new role.

The interaction between PA and staff has created even more role conflicts. As was pointed out above, the PA was accorded differential role treatment by several members of the department, which created external role conflicts for Mr. C and has caused a split within the medical staff as well. During one of the first staff meetings in August, the "pair-group" physician, Dr. P, whom Mr. C accompanied, explained the PA's role as he saw it to the other staff members. Dr. P indicated that the staff saw the PA role as "diener-supervisor" in the department and would have probably remained that, had it not been for the "pair-group" relationship. Dr. P also mentioned that the first few months were a difficult time for the PA, and Dr. P added, "I had to pull a few teeth around here in the beginning, so the PA could utilize his training." Dr. P also mentioned that all the staff, except him, are opposed to giving the PA a complete rotation with the residents. During the months from August to November, there were about twelve to fifteen staff meetings, devoted entirely to task assignments and role conflicts of the PA! The result of these conferences was the placement of the PA on partial rotation that included complete gross autopsy and microscopic work as well. Assignments of posts were made according to the demands on the residents, and in every case, Mr. C was given what appeared to be the "uninteresting" cases on paper. During February, the precedent was set to allow Mr. C to do the simple diabetic cases, but many times, the PA would end up with the most interesting cases in a pathological sense. Dr. L was made the sign-out physician for the PA on his gross autopsy and microscopic work as well. Since she worked closely with the PA, her comments are most interesting. Dr. L believed that just the anatomical aspects of the PA role should be utilized and that he should be something like a chief diener within the department. She felt that the PA was not capable of getting more responsibility since he would need a medical education to perform the final summary and interpretation. "If he gets to a point of knowing everything, he would be qualified for an MD." When the head of the department of pathology was asked what he thought the role of the PA should be, he indicated that it should be just about what it is now. The PA should relieve the pathologist from anatomical work and leave the microscopic and summary works to the residents. He also felt that the arrival of the PA with Dr. P was purely a coincidence.

Much of the interaction between PA and the staff took place during "gross conference" or "brain cutting." The doctors and residents would tell the PA to save particular organs or get a picture of certain tissue for the slide conference. At times, the PA would present his own case at these conferences and was quite capable of explaining the pathology. The result of these external role conflicts is quite evident in Mr. C's CL with the relationship he has with the department. At the beginning, his CL was quite low, and he took whatever tasks were assigned. After the resident conferences with the staff and his placement into partial rotation with the residents, Mr. C's CL began to rise, and he began to move from his latent-passive role to his manifest internalized role. After about two to three months of maintaining some role status in the department, Mr. C's microscope was removed, and the costs for the PA began to rise rapidly. It was either the removal of the microscope or the avoidance on the part of the staff and residents to introduce the PA to the new department members, which dropped Mr. C's expectations below his CL alt, and his decision to leave the department became verbalized to this researcher.

Even before Mr. C's CL alt was reached, the external role conflicts became even more divergent. Dr. L did not want him to read the microscopics while Dr. P was asking him to do a complete autopsy procedure on one of his cases. Dr. P and Mr. C would talk about the role status of the other two PAs and how the same role should be instituted at their department while Dr. J, head of anatomical, would treat the PA like a diener. I recall one time when the PA was doing an "interesting" case, and Dr. J came in and asked with a great deal of surprise, "Are you doing this one?" All in all, it was the role conflicts that reduced the PA's CL to below his CL alt and prompted Dr. P to leave the department as well. Thibaut and Kelley have indicated that the use of power can be self-defeating in a relationship, and it appears this is the case at New England Urban Hospital. The overuse of power by the staff physicians was utilized much too often, for the PA was constantly kept at the low level in order to achieve the outcomes as defined by the staff. As a result, the PA's dependence on the department declined, and the medical culture's fate control over this new role dropped. What the exact implications this power position in medicine holds over this new paramedical career are not fully known, but it appears that medicine can shape any paramedical role to its own uses. This is especially true of medicine with its low visibility and freedom from lay observation. As Freidson points out, "To be granted freedom from supervision is a mark of being trusted, of being autonomous; in short, of being a professional . . . A professional does not lower himself by snooping into the affairs of colleagues and expects his colleagues to respect the privacy of his affairs."[37] With medicine's autonomous position, it appears that this new emerging role will assume many forms depending upon the hospital setting.

Chapter Two

Work Avoidance

The concept of controlling production in any work setting has been firmly established by Everett Hughes and his students. Donald Roy's study, "Banana Time," gives us a clear concept of what this means and how it can become part of the work itself. Everett worked very closely with Roy on this study and helped formulate its direction. It was certainly inspirational to me when I sent out Darwin Crane to explore his workplace. He would come back with extensive field notes, and we would pour over them looking for what Donald Roy had described so well. What we found was beyond the type of production control Roy had discovered. It was certainly foreign to my own work experiences, and at one point, I thought Darwin was exaggerating. I met several of his friends on occasion to validate the findings, and it all appeared to be quite accurate. It wasn't until five years later that I was able to witness the same warehouse, probably even some of the same players, as I consulted on a computerized project associated with the distribution of work at the site. The last few pages address my observations and confirm what we found in the beginning.

Work avoidance is a process that can be found in all kinds of work. Even the solo practitioners of any work can find themselves avoiding various aspects of the job they find distasteful or demeaning. This paper demonstrates how the process can spread to such an extent that doing any kind of work is looked upon as unusual. It was certainly an unusual place of "work."

Work Avoidance

Everett C. Hughes has discussed the concepts of social rhythms and cycles—two categories that deal with the structuring of time, especially as they apply in a work drama. *Work time* is a term that can be applied to any aspect of the temporal structuring of an individual's work or the flow of a work rhythm within an organization. The entire area of work time can be viewed as a negotiable quality between the one doing the work and the one wanting it done, for most work is performed *for* someone rather than for the person actually completing the work tasks. Most work, therefore, is conducted under a mutual agreement between the worker and the manager, especially as it applies in the contractual sense. These negotiable arrangements can also be of a more informal nature but with the expectations of what "proper" activities should fill the worker's time.

There are, of course, numerous ways the workers can organize their time on the job. Some may even accomplish the work expected of them from management. This negotiable relationship has been the focus of various disciplines within the social sciences. However, only the sociologist is concerned with the tremendous variance that does occur, not only on the formal contractual level but the more subtle levels as well. In fact, it is this informal arrangement of work time by the workers themselves that is the focus of this paper. Others have been interested in the workers' perceptions of how their work is involved in the work time of others. Roy, 1935 observed the strategies of army-reserve-enlisted individuals as they avoided work during their weekend warriorship. This paper is concerned with the developing ideologies and strategies that are employed by the workers and supervisors during the informal process of defining work within their work organization.

There is a small body of literature that depicts the negotiable aspects within a work organization as they apply to work time besides those mentioned above. Barney Glaser has done a most interesting study of this phenomenon as it applies to the general contractor and those who employ him. The main emphasis of Glaser's work is strictly related to those negotiations of time when the contractor should be "on the job."[38]

Temporal Contingencies of Work Avoidance

This study was conducted over a period of one year using participant observation and formal interview of workers within an automobile-parts warehouse. Many of the observations were collected by my student assistant who worked full time in the parts warehouse, and I am indebted to Darwin R. Crane for his excellent observations. I am also indebted to Anselm Strauss and our many conversations concerning work time. The analysis and follow-up interviews were conducted by this writer.

All the workers in the warehouse were assigned to specific work areas, and their movements were confined to these strict physical boundaries. Management considered a worker in violation of company rules if the workers did not respect the boundaries. The two basic work groups inside the warehouse consisted of "material handlers" and "pickers." The former work group consisted of employees assigned to a specific area where their work involved the placement of automobile parts into boxes for shipping. The "pickers" were the workers assigned the task of going into the storage areas of the warehouse to retrieve parts from the numerous bins, located in varying distances, from the work benches of the material handlers. Foremen supervised the collection and packaging of the parts. These assignments were based upon territorial boundaries. Since the pickers' territories were much greater in terms of square footage (as compared to the territories of the material handlers), we find the strategies of each, as they apply to work avoidance, to differ greatly.

The avoidance of work within the warehouse ranged from partial to total avoidance. It was such a common occurrence that it became a major concern for the management and employees alike. There was always a certain amount of work that could be avoided without the threat of sanctions by management. However, there were other forms of work avoidance that did require the taking of risks by those who participated in them. This interplay between worker and supervisor in negotiating the risks involved in the avoidance of work tasks resulted in many and varied styles or strategies among the workers.

The avoidance of work became a major temporal contingency for those in the warehouse—for those doing the work and for those who watched the work get done. A great deal of each working day was consumed in avoiding work and/or the foremen, and the strategies used to accomplish this avoidance ritual depended upon a number of factors.

The main determinant of implementing a work avoidance strategy was the degree of visual supervision maintained by the supervisor. If work were performed in an open area where the supervisor could have visual accessibility, the strategy would include secret avoidance techniques. This was especially true of the material handlers' area where the tables were confined and located very close to the foremen's office area. Such close proximity to the supervisor was considered risky for displaying an open avoidance strategy. Visual accessibility by the supervisors did increase the risk-taking for the material handlers, and the strategies that emerged in this area were surreptitious in nature. The workers would control their own time while avoiding work. Time would be "seized" by the workers between steps in the work process itself. Time could be extended and controlled at a rate acceptable to those doing the work. There was a conscious group effort among the workers to be the definers of work in the material handlers' area as opposed to the foremen whose task was to be the official definer of what constituted a day's work. Definition of a "hard" worker was based upon the number of lines that a worker completed during his/her shift. A line was defined as a part placed into a particular order for shipping. The part could range in size from a radiator cab to an entire engine block. A "hard" worker was defined as someone who performed four hundred lines each eight-hour shift. This allowed the other workers to gauge their own amount of work and the risks that were involved in performing below the three-hundred-line average. The risks became greater for those doing between 120 and 180 lines each shift.

Work avoidance time was not the only time that became meaningful for the workers. "Work time" and "free time" were also important categories within the warehouse. All three uses of time varied greatly among the individual workers and among the many informal groups of workers that became identified during the course of the study. There was, however, a common theme to the structuring of time by the workers, and it always dealt with the negotiable relations between the workers and the supervisors.

To begin with, each worker accepts the job on a temporary basis and may be released by management at any time during the first ninety-day period. It was most interesting to observe and interview these temporary workers, for their work rhythms were in great contrast to the permanent employees. Because management was concerned with the performance of the temporary worker, there were more observances of their behavior by the supervisors. This close managerial scrutiny increased the work time of the temporary employees, decreasing both their free time and avoidance time. The temporary employees completed most of the work we observed during the year. It is during this ninety-day period that the employee learns to accept the definition of work time as defined by the permanent workers. It was certainly the exception for the temporary worker to continue his work pace after the probationary period, but it was most definitely altered within six months in all cases.

This change in the definition of work time by the new workers was accomplished in two ways. The first involved the awareness that there was a group definition of work. If a new employee exceeded or extended work time beyond the group-defined limits, he would be reminded of his error. If group pressure did not begin to redefine work time for the new employee, the second process would usually accomplish the task. This involved the awareness that hard work was not rewarded. Since the supervisors were held responsible for production, they were forced to use those who were willing to work harder for the most unpleasant tasks. The new worker would begin to resent his unique status as the "hard worker" after several experiences of helping the supervisors. This resentment would be the beginning of work avoider socialization. Most temporary workers were using the group definition of work time by the end of the probationary period. Shortly after the new workers attained some degree of seniority, they would begin to avoid work themselves.

Once the worker began to take up the group work rhythm, he also began to learn of the variations in "free" time and "avoidance" time. Avoidance time was the time that was carved from the workday but with the appearance that work was being performed. Avoidance time in this situation resembles Roy's "banana time" in many respects. Free time was also carved from the workday but where the workers did not have to appear to be working. Free time ranged from a management-approved period consisting of two fifteen-minute breaks during the day to unapproved time periods. Free time was valued more highly by the workers since one did not have to feign being on the job. The awareness of risk-taking by the workers for engaging in free time and avoidance time was always present. Risk-reduction strategies became an integral part of the survival knowledge of each worker. In a system where avoiding work was the norm, the survival knowledge of the workers must be extensive. Part of this knowledge included the awareness that the various uses of time were a negotiable process between the workers and the supervisors. Both the workers and the supervisors began to learn that temporal expectations were adjusted according to the various strategies used to seize free or avoidance time. Free time always involved greater risks and greater rewards. The risk-reduction strategies used for gaining free time were almost always group strategies.

Work Avoidance Careers

The use of avoidance time and free time by the workers was distinguished between "safe" careers and "risky" ones. The risky career involved high degrees of risk-taking, either individually or by a group of workers. Those involved in risky careers were given more status among the workers. Safe careers involved lower degrees of risk for the participants and also applied to both individuals and groups.

Safe Careers

The majority of the warehouse workers utilized the safe career. The major criterion that separated the safe avoiders from the risky ones was the visual accessibility, utilized by the foremen. Those areas that were open to visual supervision and where the work was performed in the open (such as in the case of the material handlers) were always considered high-risk areas for anyone contemplating a risky career. The material handlers, therefore, were representative of the safe avoidance career.

The strategies that were utilized by the low-risk employees included both individual and group strategies. Throughout the warehouse, there was a constant comparative process among the workers in order to maintain a level of production that did not deviate too much from fellow employees. This was even true of the picking routes utilized by the pickers themselves. These routes into the remote areas of the warehouse followed patterns that were fairly predictable, and we found these patterns were learned from the one who trained the new employees. The new pickers were also "helped" on occasion by other pickers when they appeared to deviate from the established way of picking the parts in the back areas.

The most common individual strategy considered nonrisky was to place "back orders" for the part requested by the dispatcher. This was usually done for heavy parts. Back orders were placed for these parts even if they did appear in the bins. Because management sometimes checked these back orders, the picker had to reduce his risk of detection by occasionally, "accidentally" dropping the part on the floor, thereby emptying the bin. On some occasions, the parts would be hidden throughout the warehouse also.

Another strategy utilized by those interested in maintaining a safe career as a picker was to hide or destroy the order cards. Stuffing them under bins, tearing them up, and flushing them down the toilet or just dropping them on the floor could accomplish this. Many times, the floors around the remote warehouse areas were visibly cluttered with such cards. If cards were lost, then the picker was not responsible for the part. This was done most of the time when the picker felt he was given a lousy "pad" or order and most of the parts on the pad consisted of heavy parts. There were many variations upon this original strategy, but the female pickers certainly had their own when it did come to picking of heavy parts. If the destroying of the order card could become too obvious to the supervisor, then a female picker could usually get another male picker to get the part for them—something male pickers would not do for each other.

Another low-risk strategy that was used by some workers consisted of knowing the habits of each of the supervisors. This knowledge allowed the workers to play supervisor against one another in terms of worker responsibility. Since this strategy required personal information of the supervisor, there developed substrategies that allowed some of the workers to maintain special relationships with the supervisors. These relationships ranged from formal to very intimate. The workers choosing friendships would use the relationship to control their own work time on occasion. One worker in particular would constantly make up stories of woe to tell his supervisor—a strategy that permitted the worker a sense of intimacy with the supervisor. Other workers would apply a strategy to gain control over the worker-foreman relationship. This control was determined by two major criteria—the power dimension of the foreman (weak or strong in their use of authority) and the nature of the relationship itself between worker and foreman (friendly or antagonistic). If the supervisor was perceived to be weak in his work demands, a worker could befriend the supervisor and play upon his role. Or if the supervisor was "demanding," the worker could deploy a more aggressive strategy to avoid work.

Getting close to the supervisor was established in several different ways. One worker loaned his supervisor $1,500. Since the supervisor was not able to get the loan through the commercial institutions, he accepted the employee's money. This strategy virtually guaranteed his immunity from harassment by the supervisor.

Another strategy some of the workers utilized to establish a cordial relationship with the supervisor was to seek counsel on personal problems. These problems could be real or imaginary. Since supervisor information was readily available through the informal information network, the problems that were brought to the supervisor were usually ones that the supervisor had already experienced. One of the supervisors had experienced a divorce, and one of his married workers would constantly discuss imaginary marital problems with him. This was particularly effective when the worker was frequently absent or late to his work. Even though this particular worker had a poor attendance record, he was never disciplined because of his empathetic relationship with his supervisor.

Making the supervisor look good was another low-risk strategy available to the workers. Upper management monitored many times the work in a particular area. This allowed an opportunity for the workers to become enemies or allies of the supervisor. The workers could choose to increase or decrease productivity, depending upon their relationship to the supervisor. If some workers decided to make the supervisor "look good," it was usually those who were facing possible disciplinary action who agreed to increased production. Not all individual strategies were low-keyed. Another common technique involved intimidating the supervisor. Even this could be used as a low-risk strategy in some cases. Harassment was a common technique utilized by the workers. A worker would complain to a point where the supervisor would eventually leave him alone. As one worker put it, "Nobody likes to get bitched at. If you keep it up long enough, he will quit asking you to do things." Intimidation was particularly effective with those foremen who were once hourly employees themselves. Since many of the employees worked with the supervisor as an equal, this was always a potential source of conflict for the new supervisor. This was particularly true of a supervisor who was promoted for political considerations and not because he was an exceptional worker. A supervisor in such a situation was on soft ground. As one worker put it, "How can he hassle me for doing the same things he used to do?"

Safe, individual work avoidance careers could not always be taken. An assertive supervisor could render the individual low-risk strategies useless. Such a supervisor demanded from the workers the necessity to rely upon group strategies in order to reduce the risks of work avoidance.

However, some individual strategies were effective in these situations and were still considered low risk in their application. One favorite strategy was to confuse the foreman by making absurd refinements or questioning legal points in the labor contract and demanding answers from the foreman. One worker put it this way, "Taking the offensive is good. Play your confidence against their fear of being stuck in the middle between the union and upper management. Play on their fear of being wrong." Such a strategy was safe up to a point, but its increased use would heighten the risks involved.

A safer strategy included attempts by the worker to encourage the supervisor to talk about himself, thereby including the supervisor into work avoidance. The less assertive supervisors required different approaches. Some were attacked personally by the worker, pointing out previous mistakes or wrongdoing by a particular supervisor. Many times, the "battle plan" would include making a joke of the work orders or giving just token response to his demands.

The varying work avoidance strategies utilized by the workers to maintain a low-risk avoidance career was numerous. In fact, they were probably as numerous as the individuals who worked in the warehouse. It was the high-risk careers that were much more visible to the observer since they required group efforts. The reason the risks were greater was because the workers utilized the strategies to gain more free time—the most valued of all temporal contingencies. Most low-risk strategies were of use to avoid work, not to seize free time. Since many of the workers were not willing to engage in the high-risk careers, most were engaged in permanent low-risk careers and were able only to avoid work by expanding the steps between the tasks that comprised the work rhythm.

Risky Careers

It was observed on many occasions that the built-in risk-taking careers were chosen as a means of decreasing the boredom surrounding the tasks in the warehouse work. Even avoidance time was not enough to keep some of the workers entertained. Seeking out free time became much more exciting and, in turn, more risky for those who did it. Because the risks were greater, the strategies that were employed became more complex. Free time became the real goal for those workers willing to share the risks involved. Risky careers, then, meant the development of group risk-reduction strategies. These strategies involved mainly the following four basic categories: *(1) covering, (2) intimidation, (3) guarding, and (4) falsifying information.*

Covering

The strategy was used with friendship groups. An individual would let it be known that he was seeking some free time and others would agree to cover for the worker. Statements to the supervisor seeking out the missing employee among the other workers included such phrases like "Oh, I just saw him two minutes ago" were common among such groups. Hiding from the supervisor for long periods of time is a risky business. Such an activity frequently involved the collusion among fellow workers. Someone in the group had to be informed of the worker's whereabouts in case the supervisor was seeking out the employee. Since free time could include sleeping, it was very important to know where the secret hiding place was located so they could awaken him in time to go home. There were many stories of sleepers not waking up on time and being locked in the warehouse.

Besides sleeping, individual free time included reading, drinking alcoholic beverages, or smoking marijuana. Some areas of the warehouse were particularly well suited for hiding, and some workers improvised beds out of foam rubber and car floor mats.

Covering for each other was the expected behavior on the part of the group members. Many of the friendship groups were highly cohesive and protective of their individual members. One good example of covering was the story of the picker who "went over the fence." This form of free time was the most valued, for one could be away from the work site altogether. When his coworkers learned that his absence had been noticed, one of them called him at the nearby bar to give him a warning. He returned to the warehouse and was seen by management. Although he was hassled for not picking up an order for three to four hours, he was not disciplined, for he was found on the premises.

Intimidating

Groups that may have used intimidation varied in size and along racial lines. The intensity of the intimidation ranged from physical force to mild verbal abuse.

Some supervisors complained that the Black workers cornered and threatened them in the remote areas of the warehouse. The supervisors also complained of Blacks filing false claims of racial harassment with the management.

Intimidation was used to control not only supervisors but the workers as well. It was the most popular group strategy used among the workers to define the pace of work. Working as a group, some workers staged a slowdown when management disciplined three workers. One entire shift stopped working over the incident. The strategy worked for the three was reinstated.

Group productivity was also maintained by intimidation. People who worked too fast found themselves the object of derogatory remarks and name-calling. Pickers who produced more than the norm had their order cards and hand trucks sabotaged to slow them. In one instance, a group of pickers hid the hand truck of one particularly fast picker so he would have to stop working.

Intimidation became more useful as a group work avoidance strategy when the company laid off fifty workers during the 1974 economic recession. The remaining workers attempted to set a new low-group standard of production to avoid further layoffs. Intimidation was always a risky business, especially when it was applied to the foremen. It was most useful in keeping the most productive workers in line, making sure such workers avoided work to a certain degree like the others. New workers became aware very quickly of this strategy, for they found themselves the target of this tactic very early in their training.

Guarding

Another high-risk group strategy that was used extensively by the workers was the practice of placing "guards" at strategic locations within the warehouse. Guarding permitted group participation of free time. The famous restroom dice game took place only when a worker was posted at the entrance so his fellow workers could be warned of approaching management. Other uses of group free time included playing of baseball, football, or a variety of other athletic competitions. Sometimes, workers would be posted so a group of workers could hide between the aisles and talk about the weekends, share a bottle of whiskey, or smoke a marijuana cigarette.

Guarding was an important, widely used strategy that allowed the workers to seize free time during their shifts. Many times, it was used to supplement the official free times (the fifteen-minute breaks). A game of cards could begin prior to the break if a guard were available. If the game proved to be exciting, several guards could be posted after the game to ensure a decent end.

Guarding was an interesting strategy. For one thing, it allowed the guards to engage in work avoidance and allowed the rest to participate in free time. The codes that were used to alert the group to danger ranged from a noise (dropping a part on the cement floor) to flashing lights (flipping the light switch in the restroom to end the dice game).

Falsification of Information

This strategy was also common among the workers. A picker's shift would begin when the dispatcher provided an IBM card for each item requested. Each card represented a "line." The picker's responsibility was to obtain the part requested from its respective location in the warehouse, place it on the hand truck, and return to the shipping area. The dispatcher maintained an activity record called a "line sheet." The line sheet listed each picker by name and divided the workday into eight separate units. The dispatcher would write down the number of lines contained in each order (in corresponding time slot), next to the name of the picker who received the order. The line sheet, then, indicated the amount of time each picker took to fill each order. Since the picker had to report back to the dispatcher after completing an order, the line sheet was effective in keeping a record of each picker's productivity.

However, group work avoidance strategies were effective in falsifying production figures. The dispatcher could be lured away from his line sheet, long enough for another worker to change the figures. This was very risky, however, and was seldom used except in extreme cases.

Workers that had had too much to drink were provided parts, and their orders were filled by their friends. This was the mildest form of falsification. The most common included the filling of back orders for one or two particular parts by all workers. This was possible when a group would ensure these parts were not in the bins, by removing them at the beginning of the shift. Falsification was a much more popular strategy several years ago, when the workers were allowed to keep records of their own productivity.

Summary

This study revealed the various uses of time by workers in a large automobile-parts warehouse in northern California. Work time, avoidance time, and free time were three categories that emerged from the data. The various strategies that were employed by individuals and groups to insure that each of these time categories was present within an eight-hour shift of each working day have been the subject of this study.

Work Avoidance: Five Years Later

This follow-up study was arranged after many meetings and the submission of several, formal written proposals to upper management. This study was conducted through Davis and Frensley Associates, not as a sociological study but as a review of the manual data processing dispatch operation. Only a few of those who read the proposal were familiar with my previous study. Since much of the work scheduling that my research assistant and I witnessed in the first study related to the dispatch activity, the follow-up study was written as a proposal for designing a computer dispatch program. This, in turn, required a systematic analysis of the dispatching tasks already utilized. This allowed me greater access to all areas of the warehouse and an opportunity to review the work avoidance strategies once again. Since I was identified as the "computer programmer," my presence among the workers was not threatening—another factor that allowed for quality data collection.

The Proposal

The main focus of study centered on the temporal aspects of work organization. My main focus was the temporal aspects of the dispatching process with possible alternatives of transferring manual procedures into a computer program. The factors that were considered for study included scheduling (e.g., shifts and task scheduling; synchronization of tasks; management of idle time; work interpretations; and their consequences) and aspects of rhythm (e.g., seasonal, weekly, and daily cycles; rotation of tasks; and work rates). The research focused on discovering the relationship between temporal factors surrounding the dispatch and other aspects of work, including worker satisfaction and impact of work on other commitments of workers. The chief means of investigation was participant observation, supplemented by intensive field interviewing in situations of theoretical interest.

Scheduling and Rhythm

Temporal factors of work can be divided into two broad classes: scheduling factors and aspects of rhythm. Problems associated with dispatching included not only the arrangement of the workweek into workdays, the familiar problems of pace of work, and the management of multiple and overlapping shifts, but also such aspects of work organization as synchronization of tasks among departments, the use of "down" or enforced idle time by both workers and management, and the impact of deadlines and other forms of time budgets. Problems of rhythm included the regularity of work tasks, the predictability of interruptions and demands for special services, rotation of workers through jobs, cycling of tasks and duties for workers, and the seasonal and other fluctuations that impacted the automobile-parts business.

While a number of studies have considered some of these factors from a sociological point of view (e.g., Roy, 1952, 1959; Blauner, 1964; Nelkin, 1970; Strauss, 1971; Weinberg, 1971; Glaser, 1973), most studies that have focused upon variables of this type have been done from the point of view of the time-and-motion studies expert or the industrial engineer. As a result, the impacts of the various temporal aspects of work organization on worker satisfaction and quality of life have been underplayed at the expense of an emphasis on economic productivity. Furthermore, there are no studies that treat a number of different temporal factors simultaneously. The major focus on temporal aspects of work from the sociological perspective has been on careers (Becker and Strauss, 1956; Hughes, 1958, 1959, 1971; Glaser, 1968 Glaser and Strauss, 1970). These studies have rarely considered the relation of other temporal aspects of work to career organization. An exception is Faulkner (1971), who devotes some time to considering these problems for the case of the professional musicians.

Those performing it as opposed to those demanding its performance have always understood the concept of work differently. Worker satisfaction and informal control over the work environment are related subjects in the distribution of tasks within a work organization. Viewing the problems from the perspective of the dispatcher (the one distributing the majority of work assignments in one particular work organization) can provide greater insight into the variety of informal arrangements that the workers use to control the scheduling and work rhythms demanded by management.

Although most social scientists would agree that understanding the temporal organization of life, and of work in particular, is a crucial aspect of any comprehensive analytical grasp of human affairs, little systematic research has been done, which leads to the formulation of useful theories of temporal organization. This study was designed as one small step in the development of a more comprehensive understanding of social, economic, and political phenomena.

The Dispatch Process

The work of a particular person appears as a series of tasks, which may be more or less interdependent upon one another and which use a variety of external arrangements to store information and equipment relating to the tasks to be performed. Tasks also have different patterns of interruptions that require the worker to stop what he is doing and begin something else.

The arrangements made in the work setting for synchronizing and scheduling all of these considerations may be internal to the task or external to it, and they may not be under the control of the worker. Some kinds of work may require a large number of different subtasks, while other kinds of work might involve the repetition of just a few essentially similar subtasks. Finally, the tasks involved may be carried out by one person or may need the cooperation and simultaneous participation of a number of people.

Variation across work settings on each of these dimensions implies a different organization of work, different temporal considerations, and different problems in maintaining an adequate balance of satisfactions in the work setting. The dispatcher must be able to perform a variety of tasks and maintain some control over the distribution of the work he is requesting from those who receive his work orders. The problem of establishing an adequate balance between worker satisfaction and job performance is a tenuous one. Establishing cooperation and coordination of tasks cannot always be realized. The result is the development of conflict between worker and management and an attempt to control the work environment, either through formal contractual arrangements, informal understandings, or both.

The Findings

The 1974-75 study discussed the notion of "work time," "free time," and "avoidance time" among the automobile-parts warehouse workers. The dispatching study allowed me access to the internal process of allocating work within the warehouse. From this perspective, I was able to verify the previous observations.

The skilled and unskilled worker ratio remained about the same—85 percent being in the unskilled group. This group, although divided into ten job classifications, comprised 75 percent of all hourly workers in the warehouse. Most of these workers were employed as stock pickers, checkers, and material handlers.

The warehouse layout remained the same in the shape of a capital E and was consisting of over four hundred thousand square feet, including the outside storage area. The foremen to workers ratio also remained the same. Eight supervisors were responsible for supervising between ten and fifteen workers each. The supervisor answered to a general supervisor and a shift superintendent. The only difference in the 1979 study was an increase in the number of security guards. Instead of three guards being present during any one shift in the warehouse, the 1979 data revealed five such security personnel. The reason for the increase in the security was revealed during the course of the study.

One of the most visual changes that occurred during the five years was the increase in female workers. Even two of the supervisory positions were held by women. This particular change was not viewed as a positive one by a majority of the male workers. Because the workers held such a negative view of management to start with, there was always a group effort, on the part of the workers, to provide a united front. In other words, the basic rule concerning work avoidance among the workers had not changed—do not volunteer information about other employees to management. So even with the increase in female employees, the male workers treated them as equals when dealing with management.

Another major difference that occurred was the establishment of a central dispatch over the work of the picker, material handler, and dispatch personnel. This allowed management an additional check between the selection process and the output process. Any discrepancies that occurred between the two dispatch centers and the central dispatch could be attributed to individual supervisors and/or employees.

The friendship groups remained the basic protective units among the workers for their work avoidance careers. Some new strategies were revealed which these groups and individuals used to slow the pace of work, but they remained as only refinements to the basic findings in the 1974 study. These will be discussed shortly.

A new source of data became available in the second study because of my position with management. Management strategies were revealed, concerning their own work avoidance and their daily battle with the workers. From this data, I was able to explore some of the causes of work avoidance and the quality of life that this form of work provided.

Safe Verses Risky Careers—A Review

The strategies that were described in the first study were still intact five years later. Some of the more "professional" work avoiders had been eliminated due to a failure in their avoidance techniques, but for the most part, the strategies remained intact. The new variations that were detected dealt mostly with the socialization process itself. These new variations consisted of: *(1) decreasing expectations, (2) the one-half principle, and (3) the cutback principle.* Each of these strategies was taught to the new employees during the first ninety days with the idea they could be used through the workers' career in the warehouse. Since the supervisors and the two dispatchers dealt directly with the workers, these strategies were constantly being employed directly at them. Their use of counter-strategies provided some interesting insights.

Decreasing Expectations

This process was used to ensure that the supervisor and the dispatcher expected less and less from an individual worker. This approach, if used correctly, was also used to guard against management personnel, increasing a person's workload in their work career. This particular approach was used as a safe avoidance career strategy, for it allowed the individual ample time to establish his/her career path.

In the beginning of a worker's career, this technique was useful as a means of feigning ignorance. If the supervisor, for example, asked a new employee to complete a specific job assignment, the worker was only responsible for what the supervisor specifically requested. If the entire assignment was expected to consist of the completion of three separate tasks and the supervisor assumed the worker to know this already, then the worker could use the steps between the tasks as a stopping point. The worker could not be held responsible for the job assignment if he did not know what the end result to be. Such behavior was used by the workers in the hope of alerting the foremen that they were "dull" or "slow" and, therefore, give the impression of not expecting too much from them in the future.

This strategy could be used in a variety of work settings even after one had been working for several months. If a worker continued to "mess up" specific assignments issued by the supervisor, especially extra assignments demanded by upper management, then a supervisor would avoid such individuals in the future. Good examples of this were observed every day. One picker, for example, who was asked by the supervisor to pick an order quickly, deliberately took longer than necessary. He claimed the part was placed in the wrong bin and had to search for it. In this case, the worker's strategy was successful, for the supervisor never asked this one picker to do something extra.

This particular strategy was most effective with the supervisors, but even the individual dispatcher was aware of its use. Some orders required a rush order from an individual auto agency. The dispatcher was aware of the diminished expectations strategy and maintained his own strategy to deal with it. The dispatcher never let it be known that the order was important.

One-Half Principle

After a worker had been on the job so long that the decreasing expectation strategy would place his job in jeopardy, he/she could employ the one-half principle. Keep in mind that this particular technique was used most often with the supervisor, for he was the one who could always make additional requests of a worker's time. Whenever a foreman made a special request, the worker could perform only half of what he was asked to do and still not be disobeying an order, for he could always use the excuse that he didn't have the time to complete the assignment. This way, the worker would not have to feign ignorance—a dangerous strategy for the experienced worker. If a worker were to disobey a direct order, he/she could be reprimanded and placed on report. If another infraction occurred within a forty-five-day period, the worker could lose their seniority and position or both. If the worker could prove he was "out of time" and not able to complete the special assignment, he could escape the supervisor's wrath.

This particular strategy was also used with the dispatcher when he assigned bulky parts on an order. If the worker saved such an order for the end of a shift, he could claim that the time was too short to return to the back of the warehouse. The dispatcher could not claim otherwise.

Cutback Principle

If given a special assignment by a supervisor, a worker could complete the job assignment but would cut back in another area. The area that was eliminated was always conspicuous enough for the supervisor to notice. This allowed the supervisor to choose which of the tasks he wanted to see completed, without the expectation that both be done.

This particular strategy was used extensively to play one supervisor against another or the dispatcher against the supervisor. If the supervisor requested a special assignment from a worker, the worker could use the excuse that another supervisor or the dispatcher was already requesting work from him. If the one requesting the work was senior to the other supervisor, the worker could choose which of the supervisor's request he would complete. By withholding his information from both of the supervisors, the worker could choose the easiest job and tell the other supervisor the reason for not completing his particular assignment.

Management Fighting Back—Foremen Strategies

One of the areas that did not appear in the first study related to the various strategies that were employed by the supervisors themselves. The supervisors were very cognizant of the fact that the work avoidance strategies were being employed. The foremen were aware of most of the work avoidance strategies that were employed by the workers.

One of the most interesting aspects of management's position was the vocabulary that was used to describe the work of the warehouse workers. *Goldbricking* was a term that was used by the foremen to explain the actions of the work avoiders. One foreman explained it in the following way: "I can't get people to work who have no motivation to do so. They work as slow as possible and not even give a shit. My job is to keep the pressure up so at least they move."

There were several strategies that management utilized to "keep up the pressure." Since the workers would not respond to urgency, the foremen had to rely upon two groups of workers, which were forced to respond to their orders: the new employees who could be released at any time during the first ninety days and those placed on a forty-five-day probation period for disciplinary action. It appeared on many occasions that without this cadre of workers, very little of the parts orders would not have been shipped from the warehouse. This, of course, reinforced the workers to avoid work once they were permitted to enter permanent status again since they resented having to do most of the work during their probationary period.

The supervisors would also utilize group strategies. Some would patrol the back of the warehouse in pairs so they could have a witness when busting an employee for a work violation. It was also safer to have another supervisor around in the back areas since some supervisors have been beaten by groups of workers in the past. The movement of the supervisors through the warehouse was the main daily strategy to keep the workers moving.

The foremen were constantly under pressure not only by the workers but from upper management also. This pressure was passed down to the workers as patrols and busts. Because the pressure was intense at times, even the foremen resorted to falsifying their employees' line counts. This was done by giving poor performers credit for some of the work done by the "captive" employees or those who actually chose to work harder than most. This prevented the foreman's supervisor from noticing that some of the workers under them were not producing. This would free the foreman from the embarrassing situation of trying to explain why he could not get some of his people to work. Such a strategy prevented the better workers of appearing in good light with upper management since their efforts were used to protect the individual foreman. The foremen in such cases never realized that such a tactic increased the work avoidance behavior of the workers since the better workers were actually punished for their efforts.

Another strategy available to the foremen was "the list." The list kept the names of those workers who had the greatest reputations for work avoidance. If such employees could not be busted by the conventional means, then the foremen placed the names of such workers on their collective list. During periods of economic recessions, these workers on the list could become "unemployed." Sometimes, this required the layoff of several good workers on the seniority list in order to eliminate those on the foremen's list.

The foremen also used security guards as a strategic weapon. During the first study, there were only three guards to a shift while the second study revealed five guards on any one shift. The reason behind this was obvious. Security personnel could also bust employees for violations such as drinking, smoking marijuana, and gambling. In fact, a security guard could make his bust stick most often at the labor board since he was considered neutral without any "axe to grind." The foremen could "set up" a person they wanted to bust by making sure a guard would be present to do the busting. The dispatchers also found themselves used by the foremen in the daily battle between management and labor. They would be requested to hold particularly difficult orders by the foremen so the foremen could issue them to their "favorite" work avoider. If they could get such a worker mad, they would have an easier time of busting them. The dispatchers would not always cooperate since they would like to save the more difficult picking jobs for their own revenge on those they thought to be goldbricking.

The Game of Work Avoidance

The work avoidance among the workers and the process of "busting" among the foremen was a constant game played out each day in the warehouse. However, it was a serious game of winners and losers, and the excitement that it generated produced a form of amusement and entertainment for both sides. Even the foremen enjoyed the battle since they too were bored with their work. As one foreman put it, "When you take away your fear of being fired, you take away your stinger. When you take away your stinger, you take away your desire. Because if you don't have to fight to live, then half of your drive is gone. If it was ever to the point where I would quit fighting the corporation, I'd quit. It wouldn't be worth it. I've got to fight them. But the game now is exciting because it's a fight every day. I could go to work tomorrow and be fired, and that's what I love about it. That's management."

No one in the warehouse identified with the product that emerged from the warehouse. One foreman explained it this way, "The workers are so alienated that they hate this place. Shit, we hate this place too. Who gives a shit about car parts? I know someone has to do it, but I know the workers really resent it. They begin to hate the corporation for giving them the job. They begin to think, 'Wow, I'm going to be doing this the rest of my life?' They get fed up with themselves for settling for it and think, 'I'm settling for this? That means that if I settle for something like this, I must be fucked, but I'm not fucked; the job's fucked. That means, the corporation is fucked for offering me this job.'"

One of the causes that was detected in both studies for this form of work avoidance behavior was the lack of incentives for the workers. There was very little upward mobility. Besides, most of the workers did not want to be promoted since they too would be placed in supervisory positions and become hated and feared by their friends. In fact, once a worker was promoted, he lost his friends almost immediately. Learning to hate management for so many years, it was a difficult adjustment for a worker to look toward the foremen as their friendship group after the promotion. Unskilled people without the opportunity of learning a skilled trade staffed most of the jobs in the warehouse. It was a place where dreams died hard and where alcohol was more popular than water, and those that had been there the longest waited for the next poker game at the next break. The only joy the workers experienced was avoiding work, and they did it the best way they knew how, by making the game exciting and dangerous and confronting the corporation together.

Chapter Three

Risk-Taking Careers

I have enjoyed very much reading your paper on "Risk Taking." I don't know that I have any suggestions to make. I can only report a number of cases that came to me by free association as I read.

Did I ever talk to you about logging? My wife's brother has been a logger up the West Coast of British Columbia, taking down from the mountain-side logs of trees that are anywhere from six to twelve feet in diameter. It is a dangerous thing. A man called a "whistle punk" blows the whistle which tells the operator of the donkey engine what to do. The donkey engine lifts huge logs from the ground and hoists them on cables up into the air and drags them into a place called "the yard" where they are loaded and sent down to the water's edge. A mistaken blow of the whistle can kill everybody by dropping a log on them. There are many contingencies of this kind. The result is that the logger, that is to say the boss logger, the owner of the company, can hire people only with the permission of the men. They know the names of the various fallers, buckers, donkey men, etc., up and down the coast. If they don't trust a man, you can't hire him. The risk is so great that the boss loses a lot of his supposed power of choosing workers.

I wonder if you have read Blanche Geer's stuff on the steel erectors; that is, the men who raise and place steel beams in high buildings. They have some very interesting attitudes about risk and about whom they can trust. She has something on how the steel men learn. Incidentally, they are usually chosen from the families of steel people. It is not so much a long training that the other workers want; they want a man who has it in his bones—that is to say, a man who is accustomed to this kind of risk as a way of life.

I have been reading Christopher Isherwoods's *Berlin Stories*. The first one is a short novel having to do with the time in Berlin just before the Nazis came. The chief character lives in some mysterious way. It turns out that he gets information from the Communists in France and delivers it to the Communists in Berlin, but he is also, at the same time, delivering material to the Nazis and to the right-wingers in France. He is playing this game of not being caught. It is a little like the illicit love affair which you mention. It has some very nice business in it of playing one risk of discovery over against other risks of discovery. The question is whether both one's clients do not really know that the man is playing it double. It turns out that they did and were making their own uses of the fact that he was double-crossing both ways. It is a good risk-taking occupation to look at.

One of the functions of fraternities in college campuses is to reduce the risk of failure of its members. They do this partly by counseling them about what courses to take, than can reduce the risk of failing almost to zero by learning just what kind of thing a particular student can do, and what he can't do. Of course, he may succeed in getting his degree at the cost of choosing his profession. The short-term risk is that of failing courses. The long-term risk is that one will not be able to choose the profession which he will take up later. While getting a degree he is also getting a record down on paper, a record that cannot be escaped from.

Personal correspondence from Everett C. Hughes (June 19, 1972), after reading the first draft of my paper on risky careers. My final version (pretty much what you find here) was presented to Everett in 1980. This version was written in the late 1990s and was written as a journal article, which was never submitted.

I have left out a very important thing. I put him [Davis] onto the whole problem of <u>risk</u>, and he has made it a major theme. I have sometimes thought of writing sociology on the point that humans are risky. They create risks for each other and then set up institutions to reduce the risk. One might say that a large part of human society is a matter of creating risks, defining them, and creating institutions to control them.

Personal correspondence from Everett Hughes to my dissertation committee members on May 7, 1978.

Introduction

I have worked three jobs that I have considered risky. My first was when I was twelve and a flagger for a crop-dusting company. A flagger's job is to provide a target for the pilot as they make the passes over the field in order to deliver the material evenly. After the plane passes overhead, delivering the material on the field, the flagger must pace off a calculated number of steps that coincides with the width of the plane and the material delivered.

Some liquids have a tendency to drift beyond the wing span, and therefore, the number of steps increases. Twelve to twenty steps were sufficient to cover enough ground for the next pass. The flaggers on each end of the field would take the same number of steps, and the pilot would know how he was doing. The material may be fertilizer, seed, herbicides, or pesticides.

I'm not quite sure what liquids were dumped on me over the three summers I did this kind of work, but one of them was considered so dangerous we had to wear rubber suits and masks, and the field was posted for several days. Dogs, cats, rabbits, birds, or anything that could walk or crawl would die if they entered such a field. I could never understand how any of them could read the posted signs. The suits we wore on such occasions were to protect the spray from making contact with our skin. I did it only once, and no one really knew I had participated in such dangerous work. That following year, I experienced half a dozen boils. I don't know if they were related to the chemical showers I was subjected to as the planes passed over my head, but I always suspected there was a connection.

My next experience with dangerous work was working with dynamite. Meandering mounds of dirt divide rice fields in California, and these are called "checks." The mounds of dirt follow the elevation or contour of the land so that water can gradually move from a high point to a lower one so the water can move through the field while the rice plants grow during the summer.

Come fall, the field must be drained prior to using the heavy harvesting equipment. The draining process can be quite slow if the existing control boxes (one at each end of the check) were used exclusively for the draining. It is necessary to open the check at several points in the middle. Since the checks are several feet wide and at least two-to-three-feet high at points, it is difficult getting equipment into the wet field to make the necessary drain hole. Using a shovel can take hours at each point. Dynamite (10% strength, which can also be used to blow tree stumps) was traditionally used to make the hole. The workers would walk through the field using the checks to walk on.

At the appropriate point, a piece of dynamite would be placed in a hole formed by the handle of a shovel. Once the shovel handle is removed from the muck, the dynamite stick could be thrust down into it with the handle once again.

The fuses, which led into the blasting cap that was driven into the dynamite and secured with tape, were cut in lengths of a foot or two, depending on how much time one thought could be out-of-harm's way. Since the fuse could even burn under water, there was never a problem in counting out the time even though you couldn't actually see the fuse. A one-foot fuse gave you about thirty to forty seconds and the two-foot fuse twice as long.

To speed up the process, one could place the longer fused stick on one side and light it and then do the same thing on the opposite side and light it. Both sides would go off about the same time, and the water could drain without a great deal of shovel work at the end. This double-stick technique was exceptionally desirable when the temperature was close to one hundred degrees, and you felt you were out in the middle of a swamp with nothing to harm if you used the double-stick method. However, this can be an exceptionally risky way of blowing checks if things go wrong.

I had chosen this method on one field one fall day and discovered what could happen when things went wrong. I had selected a check that had been in place a number of years, which was exceptionally wide and high and had an extensive growth of water grass growing on it. I had placed the longer fused dynamite stick on one side and lit it and was doing the same on the opposite with the shorter fused stick, when I discovered my matches were wet. I could have walked away and let the one side go off, but then the other stick would be buried, and I would have to dig to find it. I decided I had time to reach into my pocket and get a drier matchbox. This took at least ten to fifteen seconds, and by the time, I could light the match, I figured I had another ten seconds or so. Just then, I saw the ground come up toward me; I really didn't hear the blast first; just the ground was moving toward me. A few seconds later, I was laying on my back in the rice water with a huge chunk of mud on me. I was able to throw it off and walk away, but it did have an element of risk in it for me. So much for the two-stick method. My name was two-stick Davis for a number of years.

My third experience with risky work was driving taxi in Boston. By far, this is one of the most dangerous kinds of work due to the crime factor in American cities at the time. The latest figures indicate that there are 15.1 deaths per hundred thousand workers for cab drivers (the highest for any occupation), 9.3 deaths per hundred thousand for police officers, and 2.1 deaths per hundred thousand for bartenders. Several Boston cabbies were murdered during my two years in the city. This had been going on for several years prior to my arrival in Boston, so most of the cabs used in the various fleets on Boston streets were equipped with thick, plastic dividers, which separated the driver from the backseat passengers. A small hole permitted the passage of money between the two spaces. My risk-reduction strategy was based upon the element of trust—something Fred Davis wrote about in his experiences of taxi driving. Maybe I'll reveal them in some future paper.

Developing a typology of risk-taking careers gives us a better idea of how extensive risky work or careers can be within society. Developing risk-reduction strategies is what permits us to keep doing these kinds of activities and allows us to spread the risk out to others.

Risk-Taking Careers

This paper is the result of twenty years of informal observations, concerning people and their work. I have read the emerging literature on risk behavior since it first began to appear some twenty years ago. Two articles, which appeared in the AJS in the 1990s, especially intrigued me, and the debate generated by the articles has prompted me to put my thoughts in writing. Both Stephen Lyng (AJS 95 [January 1990], 851-86) and Eleanor Miller (AJS 96 [May 1991], 1530-1539) debate the notion of risk-taking from a variety of perspectives. However, I don't see the need to restrict a discussion of risk-taking to either a Marxist view or make it a gender/race concept. Risk is all around us in both the natural and social worlds we construct for ourselves. This paper shall provide a broad framework to include a variety of theoretical perspectives.

The purpose of this paper is to reintroduce the concept of career—a concept that I have not seen either used for a number of years in the sociological literature or applied to the area of risk-taking. The concept of "career" has been used by a number of sociologists, particularly from the Chicago school. I had the great privilege of learning about careers from Everett C. Hughes at Boston College. I learned then, and I still believe, that it is a very descriptive and powerful concept that can be used to study risk-taking behavior from a sociological perspective. I hope that greater comparative analysis will arise from viewing risk-taking in this manner.

Just a quick review of the literature on risk-taking behavior reveals a wide spectrum of topics that appear not to be related. There are articles that discuss insurance markets, environmental health risks, risk management in medicine and business organizations, cross-cultural aspects of risk-taking, attitude studies related to risk-taking in a variety of settings, foreign policy issues, which deal with the element of risk, genetic screening for health risk factors, and the list goes on and on. Barrie Thorne conducted her field research on the draft resistance movement around the Boston area, and she believes that risk-taking can even become part of the field experience.[39] I believe it is necessary to begin to categorize these diverse perspectives into a framework of risk-taking careers.

The notion of career is not related to just a work environment. For Hughes, the career is something that goes beyond work itself and fits into the natural cycles of our own lives. However, it is a term that has become quite useful in studying the kinds of work we do in society. This is why it is useful to begin looking at risk-taking from an occupational perspective.

The taking of risks is much more a sociological phenomenon than a psychological one. There is always a shared awareness of the risks, which must be confronted by the workers and their friends and families. The sharing of the risks and risk awareness has always been present in the very early literature. Let us briefly discuss this body of literature to illustrate the sociological significance of risk-taking.

The study of risk-taking literature can be traced back to its roots in the economic literature and the role of insurance in sharing the economic burdens of some risks. One of the more interesting discussions appears in an early twentieth century dissertation at Columbia University. It was here that a young economic student, Allen Herbert Willett, defined risk in the following manner:

> It is possible to think of risk either in relation to probability or in relation to uncertainty. As the degree of probability of loss increases from zero to one hundred percent, the degree of risk may be said to increase pari-passu . . . Considering risk in this sense, we find that the method by which the degree of risk may be ascertained depends upon the relative perfection of the knowledge of preceding conditions.[40]

Most sociologists would agree that such a simplistic view of human interactions described above can be misleading when applying it to real situations, even when the assumption is made that knowledge of preceding events is possible. This, of course, is not always the case, for people, who must make risky decisions, cannot always rely upon past events to help them develop new lines of action.

The game theory literature generated from the seminal work of Morgenstern and Von Newman's article, "Theory of Games and Economic Behavior," has discussed the impact of zero-sum games in social interactions.[41] Most of these studies have come from experimental psychology, where cooperation and competitive behavior among student populations is observed in situations of social interdependence. Although this tradition has produced some interesting reading, such studies are difficult to apply to real life situations, involving large numbers of people.

There have been other attempts to view the social world from a gaming perspective, apart from the laboratory studies of the psychologists. The most readable and promising approach is Anselm Strauss's work on the negotiation context (1978).[42] Risk-taking behavior involves not only psychological contingencies but sociological and political considerations, which manifest themselves in group interactions and group awareness of risks. This is why the area of risk-taking requires a sociological framework.

If we use Willett's definition of risk, we understand that there is generally a high probability of uncertainty associated with the outcome. When risk is introduced into the work environment, we can predict that the degree of risk-taking can vary substantially. Some work can be highly predictable, leaving little or no room for uncertainties to arise. An extreme example of highly predictable work would be the cloistered monk. Here we have an individual, performing tasks within an organization based upon rigid structure and predictability; little uncertainty is experienced; and little risk-taking observed. On the other hand, as we begin to look at occupational work, we will find that uncertainty and risk-taking can vary so drastically in work environments.

We have to ask the question of what is being risked by the participants in any risky situation. In order for an uncertainty to produce a risk, there must be a threat present. The three greatest threats that can produce risk-taking situations include: (1) life threatening risks, (2) risks that may damage the participant's health or reputation (thus reducing the length of time one may remain in the career), and (3) risks that may lead to monetary loss or ruin.

Any one of these risks to life, career, or money can be contingencies in many work situations. They can be present each by themselves or in various combinations. In developing a conceptual framework of risk-taking, the present classifications of professional and nonprofessional work become less important as we begin to focus on the conditions that produce risk-taking situations and the various strategies used to reduce the threats to those engaged in such careers.

Sociological Approach

A sociological framework can be applied to a number of diverse risk-taking situations that may appear not to be related when viewed from only a psychological perspective. The framework that is proposed here consists of three risk-taking categories: (1) game-career occupations, (2) game careers, and (3) high-risk careers.

Game-career occupations have built-in risks that the workers must confront on a routine basis as part of the job. Game careers, on the other hand, involve risk-taking but with no monetary compensation. A number of recreational activities are included in this category. High-risk careers differ from the other two since the participants are thrust into risk-taking situations on a mostly involuntary basis.

The three risk-taking categories are distinguished from each other in two important ways: (1) by the degree of control the participants have in reducing or controlling the risks they confront and (2) the degree of compensation (monetary or otherwise) that the participants receive in the taking of the risks. While game-career occupations are composed of risk takers who receive money as compensation, game careers develop around the taking of risks for the excitement generated from the risk-taking itself. While these distinctions may oversimplify the discussion, it is possible to state that both categories provide some compensation (psychological or monetary), and the participants can choose to remain participants. The high-risk careers differ appreciably in this regard. Not only do most high-risk career participants avoid entrance to such passage, but also they are sometimes subjected to paying for their involvement. In most cases, one enters a high-risk career only under duress, and the participants experience little or no control over the risks and their proposed solutions.

Before we begin to explore each of these in details, it is necessary to examine the distinguishing characteristics of these categories. Game careers and game-career occupations have their voluntary nature and the element of compensation. The participants of the former usually seek out the risks for the excitement generated or as risk-taking, which is culturally dictated. An example will be helpful here to illustrate the difference between the two. Driving a car for an exciting experience can be a game career, but making money, doing the same thing is a game-career occupation. It may appear, as we observe some drivers, that increasing the risks of driving is their single motivation for driving, but more scientific evidence must be collected to predict and determine the various driver classifications with regard to risk-taking behind the wheel. Insurance companies do have broad, general formulas for classifying drivers, but what the insurance companies use to predict safe drivers based upon actuarial charts, they still lack true predictability on a scientific scale.

Monetary compensation changes car driving into a more risky one, for audiences of car racing do not pay to see how slow the drivers can travel the racing course. Those professional drivers who demonstrate control over the risks are allowed to demonstrate their abilities in a racing situation. The driver of a car, therefore, does execute a high degree of control in determining the risk to his or her life. A passenger, on the other hand, is engaging in a high-risk career if the driver of the car increases the risk of an accident without the passenger's consent since the passenger cannot control any of the risk-taking from the passenger seat.

Sometimes, the risks become so great and formidable that participants must seek help in risk reduction or in learning what risks are present. This is most common in high-risk careers where the participants can exert little or no control over the situation. Such is the case with one entering an illness passage in the traditional, sociological sense. The person becomes "patient" when seeking out a health practitioner to assess the risks of a physical condition, which may be life threatening and career threatening, and in the case of Western medicine at least, may pose total financial ruin. Even those involved in game careers and game-career occupations may choose to seek additional help to insure success in risk reduction. These can be in the form of coaches, advisors, and consultants.

We can see that the sociological approach to risk-taking involves risk-reduction strategies that become important aspects of these careers. The effectiveness of these strategies to reduce the risks may even determine the length of time one can stay in their chosen career. The participants may discover that all those sharing the risks may formulate strategies. Or people may seek out those who may be trained in assessing risks and developing strategies independently of those who directly confront the risks.

Everett Hughes believes that age is an important factor when observing all careers, for age may determine one's ability to remain in that career. Edward Gross also makes this point in referring to occupations in the following quote:

> At the other end of the career, it may be necessary to force persons out. Sometimes, this is needed to keep alive the upward mobile hopes of others further down, or the person may himself refuse to recognize that he is no longer capable of carrying on as usual because of aging—as in the case of persons in sports, airline pilots, prostitutes, and many types of criminals.[43]

It is interesting to note that Gross's description of occupations, which force members out or make it explicit to the worker that they may no longer be capable of the routine because of aging, can be classified as game-career occupations.

It appears that age can be a factor for two reasons: (1) having more experience, e.g., greater age, can enhance one's ability to reduce the risks associated in some game careers and game-career occupations and (2) growing old may decrease one's risk-reduction abilities. While athletes (both professional and amateur) may experience a reduction in their ability to control the risks of injury to themselves or career, as they grow older, the aging process may enhance one's ability to reduce risks such as in the case of the aged lawyer or physician. Of course, there are those around to remind the individual their age and experience may no longer be an asset, as illustrated by Everett Hughes's anecdote about the aged surgeon. A young physician turned to another younger colleague while observing the surgical technique of the head surgeon and said, "Did you see the old man's hand shake?"

This is certainly one area where more research on the impact of age on decision making is needed. Other questions come to mind here also. How many occupations are there where people get in and out as quickly as possible, either for quick profits, fame, or as stepping stones for other careers? Do careers that have high degrees of risk-taking sour more quickly than low-risk careers, where some degree of stability and security exists? It would be interesting to see the types of careers that last only as long as one's ability to reduce the risks is intact.

Game-Career Occupations

Edward Gross' above quote listed some occupations that can be classified in this category. There are a number of occupations that can be listed here. Some of these have been discussed in the literature. These include *The Racing Game* by Scott; *The Professional Soldier* by Janowitz; *The Fisherman* by Tunstall; *The Hollywood Studio Musicians* by Faulkner; *The Professional Thief* by Sutherland; and *Der Man mit den Messern* by Boll. These are all risky occupations that can force the workers to participate in collective decision making to reduce or control the risks involved.

There are three game-career occupations that will be used here to illustrate some important aspects of this category. There are a number of occupations in professional sports that are certainly risk related. Farming is another occupation that produces scores of risk-taking examples that illustrate the extent of this category. The last example of mining is the most obvious type of work that falls into this classification system.

Professional athletes participate in gaming situations for a living, and the risks they encounter can lead to the loss of their careers and money. In extreme cases, the athletes can lose their lives. Athletes quickly learn the risks and apply individual and group strategies to reduce them. Even though the risks can differ among the various sports, there are risk contingencies common to all. It appears that the greater the risk-taking, the greater the excitement, which is generated and carried over to the audience of these events. Bullfighters literally place their life on the line to the screaming delight of the fans. So do race car drivers. These risks can become quite public to the horror and thrill of those who witness fatal mistakes.

Although the life threatening risks appear to get much attention, the athlete must deal with the less obvious risks that relate to them, staying in the career. Timing and agility are common contingencies that can increase such risks. Sometimes, these risks can fluctuate in one's individual career or for the entire group, as in the case of team sports. *Slumps* is a term in sports, which is generally used to describe these kinds of career-threatening risks. Some individuals (and entire teams) may lose their ability to reduce the risks and may cut short their career if their timing and agility skills increase the risks involved instead of decreasing them.

This brings up an interesting point. There is no doubt that some people in game-career occupations do experience slumps, and it is almost a universal phenomenon. But what about other game-career occupations, which do not have the public scrutiny which exists in professional sports and where the term is widely applied? Do physicians and lawyers (two kinds of work where risk-taking is an everyday reality) have slumps? If they do, how are they handled and how long do they last? In professional sports, some athletes experience slumps that may last weeks or months and may herald the end of their career. Can lawyers and surgeons experience the same kind of slumps, when their timing and agility are no longer adequate to reduce the risks that they encounter?

Another factor that can occur in professional sports (which may also be true of other occupations in this category) is the role of the audience in ascertaining the quality of the performance. Sometimes, the audience can influence the outcome of an athletic event, and the risk-sharing goes beyond the individual and the team itself. The audience can contribute to building of reputations for those who demonstrate great skill in risk reduction. The relationship that exists between the professional game players and their audiences is another area of game-career occupations that is ripe for further research.

Farming is another example of this kind of work. There is no secret to the risks which farmers must face on a seasonal basis. The federal price support programs of the United States and Europe are bureaucratic proof that the risks of farming are great. Crop failures and bumper crops can both spell ruin for the farmer in the market place. Farmers confront insects, weather, plant diseases, floods, droughts, poor soil conditions, weak market prices, and extremes in temperature, so the risk of failure is always present. All cultures approach these risks in different ways, and their risk-reduction strategies reflect this. While farmers in Western cultures rely upon scientific information and technology to control some of these risks (especially in the development of fertilizers, pesticides, and fungicides), the weather is still a risk factor where control is lacking. But even in the United States, where innovative technology is prolific, farming still remains a risky occupation.

In societies where scientific strategies are lacking, the risks for the farmer and the consumer are even greater. We begin to see new strategies developed and applied in the hopes of reducing the risks. In Dobu, for example, the men may grow the yams (the staple crop), but only the women possess the magical power to entice the yam seeds from the other men's gardens.[44] We can see from this example how cultural factors can influence the degree of uncertainty and the various means which people create to reduce this uncertainty. The Dobuan must face crop failures and explain them away just as the American farmer does. While one strategy may be magical and the other based upon science, all cultures try to control the risks associated with food production.

What can we learn about risk-taking from the farmer? Again, we are impressed with the group strategies, which appear to dominate the risk-reduction effort in the growing of food. Because the risk of failure can go beyond the farmer and impact the entire society, we see that the group effort to reduce the risks can be quite complex and involves numerous occupations, which fall outside the game-career occupation framework. These support occupations may not be risk producing for the participants but are important in finding strategies that can assist those who must face the risks. Therefore, to understand game-career occupations, we must observe the entire social world that may lend support to it. This may be true for most game-career occupations. One of the more interesting studies of risk-taking, which utilizes this approach, was conducted on the energy industries. All the risk of accidents, disease, and death of energy occupations, and occupations associated with energy production, were calculated and compared to producing a standard unit of energy (a megawatt year). The results indicate that coal, oil, and solar energy are more risk producing than nuclear energy, when occupational man days lost per megawatt year are determined over the lifetime of a system.[45]

Mining is the third occupation that will be examined since it is notoriously dangerous work. Again we will see the importance of group strategies. During the 1975 mining disaster in Idaho, the daughter of one trapped miner was interviewed. She appeared to be very hopeful that her father was still alive since she indicated, "He's worked in the mine all his life, and he knows all about keeping alive." What she meant was that her father knew the geography of the mine, in terms of airshafts and survival supplies, and was able to reduce the risks of poison gas from this knowledge.

From our discussion of the professional athlete and the farmer, we can begin to see a pattern develop, which can be applied to understanding mining as well. Miners' careers are dependent upon their ability to develop both individual and group strategies. This is how they can survive such hazardous work. We need to learn more about the other occupations that lend support to the miners through developing risk-reduction technologies. These risk-reduction strategies will vary from one culture to another just like the farming example. Miners of South American cultures have developed elaborate, magic and religious rituals to reduce their risks of death while U.S. miners rely more upon technological ones.[46]

As more research is conducted on game-career occupations, we will be able to expand our understanding of how these risk-reduction strategy decisions become formulated and implemented and how they may change over time.

Game Careers

Game careers permit the participant to **voluntarily** engage in risk-taking without monetary compensation. The many examples

Stephen Lyng used in his AJS article to demonstrate "edgework" fit nicely into this category. Driving a car is one example, perhaps the most familiar type of game career. Automobile owners, to spread the financial risks, spend millions of dollars each year on insurance. In fact, this could possibly be the most commonly shared risk in modern society. The many thousands who die each year driving a car make this activity a truly risk-taking adventure.

Another popular activity that can be studied from a game-career perspective is gambling. Herbert Block has some insight into this interesting risk-taking behavior that is applicable here.

> In summary, gambling provides a function in well-organized societies where the stress of competition (with its lack of predictability) is great, and where, in contrast, the regimen of economic and social life is rigorous. Such a society, placing a premium upon "risk" and "taking a chance," provides through gambling an outlet for many individuals who, hedged in by social restriction and limited or no opportunity, would otherwise find little satisfaction for the need for new experience and pecuniary success. This penchant for taking a chance is expressed in the popular cliché: "Why not? What have you got to lose?"[47]

Millions of people spend billions of dollars each year betting on horses, athletes, lotteries, and the numerous games in gambling casinos, where people wager money for the thrill of it and the chance to win more money. A small percentage of these people actually make a living doing this and treat the career as an occupation. For most people, however, this form of risk-taking is engaged in for the excitement generated, just as most game careers are used in this manner.

One of the most insightful descriptions of a game career is Clifford Geertz's paper on the Balinese cockfight. He makes the point that the Balinese rarely, if ever, rely upon the betting in cockfights to maintain their living.

> This, I must stress immediately, is not to say that money does not matter, or that the Balinese is no more concerned about losing five hundred ringgits than fifteen. Such a conclusion would be absurd. It is because money does, in

this hardly unmaterialistic society, matter and matter very much that the more of it one risks the more of a lot of other things, such as one's pride, one's poise, one's disposition, one's masculinity, one also risks, again only momentarily but again very publicly as well.[48]

This is the game quality of the cockfight. Geertz gives a very good account of some of the strategies the Balinese have developed to reduce the risks they assume to maintain their money and honor.

In addition to the above examples of game careers, there are scores of activities that can be classified in this category. Anything one does "just for the fun of it" usually involves the taking of some calculated risks. Skiing, sky diving, hang gliding, flying, skin diving, mountain climbing, and surfing are just a few examples of game careers. The risk-reduction strategies used by the participants have yet to be studied, but I'm sure they are not all individualistic in nature.

Not all game careers are sports activities. One such activity where risk-taking and the generation of excitement are both very high is the extramarital affair. There are definite risks that enter into an affair that may lead to the culmination of the marriage (career) and loss of money, and in some extreme cases, the life of one or both of the participants may also be terminated by the jealous party.

The affair brings to light an important dimension of risk-taking careers that can apply to all three types of risk-taking careers. This dimension involves the open or closed awareness context as described by Strauss in his work on hospitals.[49] Some people keep the fact they are taking risks a secret while others may choose to be open about the dangers they encounter. Not all risk takers can choose a closed-awareness context since some careers are known for their high-risk activities. However, there are occasions when information may be withheld from outsiders in order to keep all occurrences of risk-taking from becoming public. I found this to be true of cab drivers when I was driving for a cab company in Boston. Some were very reluctant to share with their families the exact number of robberies that took place in their city. I would also imagine that very few surgeons discuss the risks associated with the making of mistakes in the operating room (mistakes that could lead to malpractice) with family and friends. Policemen and firemen may also choose to keep "close calls" to themselves.

Before discussing the high-risk careers, it is hoped that the reader has some notion as to the similarities and differences between a game career and the game-career occupation. Game careers are quickly recognizable by their lack of monetary compensation and are recognized by others that the risk-reduction strategies require skill and/or cunning.

High-Risk Careers

Many times, these kinds of risky careers are entered involuntarily by the participants. For this reason, there may be the need to consult others who can assess the risks and provide risk-reduction strategies. Illness is certainly one of the more obvious examples. People get sick and need physicians to assist them through their illness.

The passage of a person through the legal system can certainly involve life, career, and monetary risks, and frequently do so. Charles Dickens's *Bleak House* comes to mind here. Very few individuals have the knowledge necessary to meet the potential risks of a law suit or criminal charge. A lawyer is hired because it is assumed that they will be able to determine the best risk-reduction strategies.

Flying on commercial airlines is another example that can apply here. We may get into trouble, trying to force an "involuntary" prerequisite on this type of activity since most people do choose to walk on the plane. The important point of any high-risk career is the lack of control over the many risks that can be associated with the activity.

It is no secret that flying can become a risky business, especially flying in busy (risky) corridors above our major cities. Because we choose to walk aboard the plane, we do so, knowing that there are people qualified to make the aircraft safe and risk free. In order to get people to fly, airline companies have had to spend a great deal of money, hiring people to insure some level of "safety" and insure that people can trust the company to produce a risk-free flight.

There are a number of occupations that make up the risk-reduction team. We may have to take the risks associated with flying, but we assume there are qualified workers who reduce those risks substantially. Some of these occupations keep the equipment from falling apart, keep it on track, and assist in the taking off and landing in a coordinated fashion. So there are a number of game-career occupations that assist the high-risk career participant to get through their brief flying career with a minimum of risk to their life.

Summary

The focus on risk-taking has traditionally taken place in isolated conditions, using student populations and economic theory models. Valuable insights have emerged from this form of research, especially in psychological and social psychological studies that emphasize mathematical models. However, sociologists have only recently begun to examine the sociological contingencies that contribute to risk-taking, and this paper attempts to expand the sociological approach in this area.

The three types of risk-taking careers discussed here have similarities and differences that can be used for comparative analysis. The participants of all three careers engage in risk-reduction strategies that protect them from losses. Most of the time, these strategies are group related and applied through joint action. Occupations and professions that become part of the risk-reduction effort support some of these careers. Driving a car (a game career in this context) is risky, but it is not only the driver who is responsible for risk-reduction strategies.

Car designers, highway engineers, legislators, law enforcement agencies, licensing agencies, and educators all contribute to reduce the risks of driving. It is truly a sociological problem, in conjunction with the psychology of the driver. The same can be said of being a passenger in the same car or a commercial airliner (both high-risk careers). An entire network of specialists who may assist the participants in their risky passage can surround some of these high-risk careers. Illness was the example used to illustrate this.

What this suggests is a very complex network of decision making and information assessing, taking place among a variety of risk-taking careers to reduce the risks that are generated from living in a society, especially one whose technology can generate multiple risks. More qualitative and quantitative sociological studies on these types of risk-taking careers will allow a greater understanding of how these risk-reduction strategies become formulated and implemented, not just by those who must confront the risks, but also by those who assist those who do.

Chapter Four

Work-Arounds and Organizational Flexibility

This was first presented at the seventy-ninth annual meetings of the American Sociological Association in San Antonio, Texas, in 1984.

Researchers whose chosen concerns are with the development of substantive negotiation (whether labor bargaining, economic transactions, diplomatic negotiation, and so on) are currently more likely to make major contributions to the development of a general theory of negotiation; *but certainly any researcher into substantive phenomena might make a useful contribution, provided he or she is interested in that particular theoretical enterprise. Perhaps the latter researchers can then make very interesting contributions precisely because their data will be drawn from non traditional areas concerning the analysis of negotiation.* (Anselm Strauss, *Negotiations*, pp. 244-245)

After several years of working in a variety of occupations and different organizational settings, I have begun to observe how people work around their fellow workers in an effort to accomplish assigned tasks. This paper will introduce this kind of organizational behavior and describe the various conditions that give rise to it. I will also introduce the importance of this kind of behavior to organizational change and organizational theory.

Every organization attempts to control the individual worker as well as entire group behavior, e.g., departments, branch offices, etc. Most of this control emerges from the formal task structure imposed by management. Such a structure defines the specific kind of work expected from employees. Organizational theorists have discussed the formal organizational structure and its impact on work production since sociology emerged as a separate discipline. Other sociological theorists have described the importance of the informal structure and its impact on the worker. However, the literature devoted to both of these perspectives is lacking on the issue of how people encounter resistance and attempt to get around it while attempting to get their work completed. Workers do encounter resistance in completing their formal tasks, and they do develop ways to avoid such barriers. This resistance I shall call "work blocks" and the resulting behavior, which may arise in such situations, I shall call "work-arounds." Observing each of these can enable us to address an issue glossed over by the literature on either the formal or the informal structure.

Students of organizations know the importance of the informal organization in moving information (usually labeled as "rumors") across formal organizational lines of communication, in developing what many may call "group morale," and to use Keith Davis's phrase, "to fill in gaps in a manager's abilities." However, no one has devoted much time in analyzing how people work around others, the conditions that give rise to it, or the consequences that confront the workers or the organization when, and if, these work-around arrangements are discovered. One of the important theoretical considerations that must be addressed concerning the consequences of work-arounds is the change that can result to the organization itself. As sociologists, especially those coming from a symbolic interactionist perspective, we know that organizations are not only human products but also ongoing human productions. It is human interaction that gives rise to not only the social order but also to the ultimate demise of what passes as social order at any one time.

We view organizational change quite differently from those who emphasize the formal over the informal structure. I am certainly not the first to describe the phenomenon of working around people in a formal organizational setting. Goffman (*Asylums*, 1961) addresses the issue when he uses the term *secondary adjustments* to describe inmate behavior in total institutions. However, as Strauss (*Negotiations,* 1978) points out, Goffman fails to address the issue of change in his discussion of secondary adjustments and their impact on the formal structure. "In his [Goffman's] analysis, the personnel are mainly acting, most of the time, to maintain the coercive order, and the inmates are either playing by the rules, both explicit and implicit, or acting around the margins of those rules. Their actions may or may not disrupt the ongoing order of events, but certainly they do not, ultimately, shape anew the nature of social order of the total institution itself."

It is my belief that work-arounds can and do change the formal organizational structure in both obvious and subtle ways. Work-arounds keep the formal structure flexible—a situation that can give the appearance that the formal structure may be effective when, in actuality, the workers are making the organization work in spite of itself. Once the work-arounds become so permanent and obvious to all concerned, the formal structure itself can be altered dramatically. Let us explore the conditions that can give workers the motivation to work around others if they find difficulty in working through them as a formal structure may dictate.

Conditions That Give Rise to Work-Arounds

There is probably no one permanent formal or informal structure, maintaining itself over a continuing length of time in any organization. A better description of work in general is the weaving in and out of the formal to informal rules and, back again, depending on the circumstances of the workers. The result is various hidden kinds of work.

People have a way of moving in and out of formal arrangements for a variety of reasons. Two examples come to mind here. One is Donald Roy's article "Banana Time," and the other is Robert Faulkner's "Dilemmas in Commercial Work." Roy discusses how the informal structure can help in making routine work more meaningful for the participants, and Faulkner discusses how unpredictable work can become routinized through an informal arrangement.

Both Roy and Faulkner discuss the importance of informal arrangements at work, and both deal with hidden work arrangements, but they both differ from me in their approach to informal structures. Roy discusses the importance of the informal structure in building recognition and satisfaction in a routinized setting. Faulkner discusses the subtleties of working with filmmakers who have little or no knowledge of music and therefore must work around producers and directors in such a way as to get the job done, without running into trouble with the filmmakers. Faulkner does address this issue but only with reference to a one-on-one relationship between the composer and the filmmaker. The larger studio organization is really not considered in Faulkner's work. My focus here is to explore the informal structure, whereby some of the workers see the need to move their work by others in order to get their own work accomplished but in a way appears to be using the formal structure.

Let me distinguish here between hidden kinds of work and hidden kinds of activity. Avoiding work is an activity (see chapter one) that can occur in work organizations at the informal level, where the participants attempt to avoid detection. This is different from "hidden work" where the worker is actually attempting to get his job done by avoiding some people in his formal structure. Another example of a hidden activity would be the accountants attempting to steal from the organization that employs them. They may utilize strategies to hide their activity, but the work does not fit into the formal objectives. The tasks that become completed in work-around arrangements are tasks that are sanctioned by the formal organization but not in a formal organizational way.

All organizations, both large and small, have a formal division of labor that results in a series of task structures that employees are expected to perform. Some tasks require the cooperation of a coordinated work team, whereby the work of one worker is completed before the work task can continue with another worker. This allows the completed task of one worker to become the "raw material" for yet another worker. Any delays in the flow of work can delay the next step in the task structure. When the flow of work becomes disrupted or blocked, especially when this occurs quite frequently, the workers below and above the work blockage may engage in work-arounds.

There are at least three conditions that may cause work to be delayed or blocked, at points within an organization. These include interactional, situational, and structural blocks. Interactional blocks may result from at least two sources: spatial separation of the workers that may disrupt the formal lines of communication or personality clashes that can also produce blocks in the flow of work. Sociologists have investigated these kinds of blocks since Moreno's sociometry and the rankings of likes and dislikes of people within the organization. Personality conflicts are probably fairly common in the workplace, but when it is used to actually block another worker's job, then it becomes an interactional block.

Situational blocks are different. These include incompetent workers situated up or down the flow of work. The raw product received as a completed task of an incompetent worker can result in problems for the worker who receives it next. If complaints within the formal structure do not produce changes to alter this situation, then the frustrated worker may seek out ways to establish work-around arrangements. The inferior product must either be returned up the flow to be corrected or corrected by those who receive it. If passed down to other workers in its errant state, even though corrected, others may alter it on the downstream side. Incompetent workers, therefore, generally cause situational blocks.

Structural blocks can occur and impact work at all levels within the organization and may disrupt the flow of work adversely. Among the structural blocks are those arising from organizational policies and politics. Both policies and politics can (1) influence the allocation of resources to various departments so the completion of work can become problematic and (2) set in place political blocks and power struggles that may place workers in losing situations.

Strategies for Work-Arounds

The various kinds of blocks a worker may encounter do not always lead to a work-around situation. Frustration, stress, and rumors may emerge from the worker(s) who choose to "put up with" the blocks. However, when workers do define their work as blocked and see a way around such a block as either a practical necessity or politically feasible, then strategies can emerge to accomplish the work-around.

Work-arounds require two types of strategies to be effective. One involves getting the work completed. Since creating a work-around usually takes two workers (one on either side of the block), a protective strategy is also needed to ensure secrecy. Negotiating a protective strategy among the workers will depend on the frequency of the block, whether it be temporary or permanent.

Interactional, situational, or structural blocks can be permanent or temporary, depending upon such factors as turnover of personnel, redesign of office space, and rate of organizational growth. In organizations where the turnover rate is low, specific interactional and situational blocks may be very permanent. This is in contrast to organizations that are growing and forcing changes in personnel. Fast—growing organizations still produce situations where work-arounds are negotiated to get the work done and a protective strategy established to keep it secret, but there may be the temptation by the workers, so see the blocks as only temporary, and they will disappear if one just waits long enough for things to change.

Negotiating Alliances

This is the first task a worker must accomplish so the work-around will be successful. Whether the work block is temporary or permanent, the alliances must be formed to carry out the plan of getting the work done and to keep it secret. Some of the alliances may get formed and used frequently, while others get formed and remain in place and used only infrequently since the protective strategy may require too many workers. Some work-arounds may require only temporary alliances, during an "emergency" for example, and may never be used again.

The protective strategies used to mask the work-arounds may require more time to negotiate and be more complex than just establishing an alliance around a block. The masking activity may require the recruitment of workers outside the work-around itself since some may become aware that work is diverted, and the allies on each side of the block will need to negotiate with others to keep the work-around secret.

Building alliances to protect a work-around strategy can be stressful and risky for all concerned. There can be negative consequences to establishing work-arounds in the first place, which is why protective strategies become necessary. However, allies may begin to defect from a work-around if they feel it may be detected. This brings us to the final discussion, concerning work-arounds in the workplace—the consequences of engaging in this kind of alliance for the workers and to the organization itself.

Consequences of Work-Arounds

There are at least two major consequences to be considered. There can be negative consequences for the workers who choose to engage in a work-around, and there can be consequences for the formal organization also.

The workers can probably look forward to at least four scenarios, when contemplating forming a work-around or attempting to form an alliance for one. Since the workers are engaging in hidden work activities, they can hope to be successful in getting their work done without being detected. The other three consequences deal with being detected by those in authority of the formal structure. There is the possibility of being detected without any negative action against the employees. The situation is addressed, ignored, or looked upon as a mistake. There is also the scenario where the workers are detected and reprimanded or even terminated if they continue the practice. There is even the possibility of being detected, the practice halted, and then building a different alliance and continuing the work-around. Without adequate data, worker consequences cannot be addressed beyond what appears to be the logical sequences of being detected in an unauthorized practice within the formal organizational structure.

It may be more interesting to contemplate the theoretical consequences of work-arounds for the formal organization. One major consequence of work-arounds for the formal organizations may be for some people to take credit for getting their work completed, when others are doing it for them through the work-around process. Implicit in this discussion is a view of organizations that permit a more flexible structure to emerge from the more formal and rigid one. By observing how people work around others in a formal setting, we can begin to see how organizations (and the people who comprise them) are not just acting out behaviors but creating new ways to get things done. People do find creative ways to solve their problems at work and so, too, do organizations. However, some solutions may remain hidden to those dominating and controlling the formal structure, and only through sociological research may we be able to understand how organizations remain flexible under highly controlled conditions.

Chapter Five

Information Assessment Work

In the late 1930s, throughout the 1940s, and into the 1950s, several of us at the University of Chicago were engaged in studies of industry. In 1939, I began to teach a course on professions . . . I soon changed the name of the course to "The sociology of work," both to overcome to some extent the constant preoccupation with upward mobility of occupations and also to include studies of a greater variety of occupations and problems. A great many students wrote papers on the occupations of their fathers, their kin, and even on their own . . . The contingencies which face people as they run their life-cycle, their career at work, turned out to be a constant theme. The great variety of students and of occupations and work situations studied stimulated the search for and the finding of common themes . . . If those students—who studied janitors, factory workers, furriers and the like—compared the lowly with the proud, it was not degrading of the noble, but an ennobling of what some might have considered less than noble (Hughes, 1984, *The Sociological Eye*, "The Humble and the Proud," pp. 418-420).

This chapter was originally ninety-five pages of my dissertation, which I have edited to reflect the essence of the topic. It was rewritten for a journal article many years ago, but that never got sent, so it appears here for the first time in print.

Author's Note

All work involves some amount of information assessment. Some work, however, is especially dedicated to collecting, storing, retrieving, moving, protecting, and/or assessing information in very specific ways.

The various occupations and professions that perform this kind of work will be the focus of this paper.

Information is constantly moving through organizations in the process of carrying on and completing work tasks. Some of this information is moved into the organization from the outside, some may be created from within, and there is the likelihood of information emerging from the organization in one form or another as the work gets done. The result is a continuous flow of information in, through, and out of an organization. This flow may consist of four major components: developing the flow, monitoring it, keeping the flow steady, and describing. Let us look at each of these in turn.

Developing the Flow

An information flow is developed by those occupations that seek out sources and begin feeding the information into the organization. Some sources can be as overt as the public library, while others are much more difficult to locate. Overt and covert become two important contingencies in developing a flow. The numerous occupations that develop information flows in organizations can all be categorized as "information scouts" for the purposes of this paper. Information scouts, as they confront both willing and unwilling sources, begin to develop strategies that permit the extraction of "proper" information.

Let us take a few organizations and see how information flows develop. This will permit a better understanding of the work performed by information scouts within organizations. People who are ill will seek out a physician who is trained in scouting out the right information, even if this information is "hidden" within one's body. These scouting techniques are looked upon within the profession as diagnostic methodologies. Whatever they are called, the scouting effort by a physician begins to produce a flow of information from the patient source.

Other work organizations have similar ways of collecting information. Law firms, or even solo practitioners, begin to collect information after the client walks through the door. Although the client or patient may remain the primary sources of information in both kinds of work, other sources may still be sought out. Law or medical libraries can be additional sources of information. Other people may be asked to testify in court in law cases, or relatives of a patient may be additional sources for the doctors or nurses. Even insurance companies or public agencies may begin to volunteer information to a hospital once a flow of information begins to develop around a patient.

Let us return to the scouting process itself. Some scouts are clear about the information they want. Others may have to develop tactics that resemble "fishing expeditions." Take, for example, the people who run airport security systems. The metal detectors and X-ray machines are nets to catch specific information—the presence of weapons and/or explosive devices.

While accountants may be fairly certain about information they want, private investigators, on the other hand, and even investigative reporters, may find themselves at a loss for specific sources and must devise ways to collect information they think they need to complete an investigation. This is why sources may be either overt or covert. So accountants can be examples of overt scouts, and the private investigators is best described as a covert scout.

Overt scouts seeking overt sources are in great abundance in almost all societies. Uniformed police and security personnel are obvious examples. They make a great effort in being overt by wearing uniforms and badges and carrying identification of official status. Because they are so overt and have a "license to act," they are able to develop a flow of information quite quickly. The following quote exemplifies this:

> Whenever there is an increase in the weekly totals of crime reported, the men (sic) are urged, but not ordered, to be more 'aggressive' on patrol and to 'increase the number and quality of vehicle and pedestrian stops' they make. This attitude is motivated by the belief that the more activity a man is involved in scanning the people and cars about him, the more likely he is to detect and prevent crime. (Rubinstein, 1973, p. 47)

Physicians and nurses also engage in overt scouting and have a license to act. They, too, can quickly establish a flow of information through questioning and diagnostic testing. The sources can be both willing and unwilling, which is very similar to the police situation.

The credit card industry provides us yet another example of overt scouts seeking overt sources—their customers. Here, the potential customer provides the information to the employee/scout, and others in the organization can use this initial information to seek other more covert sources in order to determine the accuracy of the data. Since the various occupations that compose this kind of data collection have not been studied from this perspective, it might be helpful if we give them a name that describes the kind of work they do. *Public surveillance* scouts is a useful term since there is a great amount of information being collected by a variety of occupations and professions that fit this description. With the increase of credit card use in the United States, today comes an increase in the occupations associated with information collection. Credit grantors have thousands of employees who collect and verify information on a daily basis. One of the best sociological discussions of this form of information scouting is James B. Rule's book, *Private Lives and Public Surveillance*. Rule points out that as more and more information on individuals is collected and stored on computers in a variety of organizations, there is a greater chance for this information to be used for purposes other than was originally intended. Rule points out the relationship between increased credit card use and increased surveillance:

> But the need for centralization in consumer credit reporting stems not only from the increasing dispersion of individual consumer's account data but also from the increased residential mobility of credit card users themselves . . . For centralization makes it easy both to incorporate data on or from any point within the system's area of coverage, and to have recourse to such data without necessarily knowing where the client resides at the time. Here as elsewhere, growth in the scale of social structure draws mass surveillance itself into increasingly large-scale organizations. (Rule, 1974, p. 305)

The insurance industry provides another example of public surveillance scouts when it comes to information collection. Insurance is issued by two broad categories: life and health and property and liability. Once the customer provides the information to the insurance agent, the organization passes it through a variety of other sources to verify it. An insurance organization may verify information by crosschecking with available credit bureaus, the Medical Information Bureau (MIB), the Impairment Bureau (usually for life and health insurance and the loss indexes on the property and liability side), Fire Marshall Reporting Service, the Burglary and Theft Loss Index, the National Automobile

Theft Bureau, and the Index System. There is also the American Insurance Association (AIA) that provides service bureaus to members, and in some cases to nonmembers, which seek out and maintain information on prior loss records, claim records, and financial information related to property value and liability coverage. The Fire Marshall Reporting Service is used only for the processing of claims. It is viewed as a check for prior loss on claimants, where arson is suspected. The same is true for the Burglary and Theft Loss Index. It is maintained to check for fraudulent claims. The National Automobile Theft Bureau maintains files on all stolen and salvaged vehicles.

Trying to conceal information from those seeking it can be a risky business in itself. Patients do it to doctors, criminals do it to the police, and clients from their lawyers. This is a major contingency in any work that collects information to assess. Although secrecy was one of the first topics introduced to American sociologists through Simmel, little has been done since to understand the extent and usage of secrecy in human affairs. Since Simmel introduced this topic, I will let his words explain this important phenomena:

> The secret . . . is one of man's greatest achievements . . . The secret offers, so to speak, the possibility of a second world alongside the manifest world; and the latter is decisively influenced by the former. (Wolff, 1964, p. 330)

Another quote from Simmel is applicable today to illustrate the relationship between overt scouts and covert sources:

> Our modern life is based on a much larger extent than ever is usually realized upon the faith in the honesty of the other. Examples are our economy, which becomes more and more a credit economy, or our science, in which most scholars must use innumerable results of other scientists that they cannot examine. We base our greatest decisions on a complex system of conceptions, most of which presuppose the confidence that we will not be betrayed. Under modern conditions, the lie, therefore, becomes something much more devastating than it was earlier, something that questions the very foundations of our life. If among ourselves today, the lie were as negligible a sin as it was among the Greek gods, the Jewish patriarchs, or

the south Seas Islanders; and if we were not deterred from it by the utmost severity of the moral law; then the organization of modern life would be simply impossible; for, modern life is a "credit economy" in a much broader than a strictly economic sense. (Wolff, 1964, p. 313)

Computer fraud is a most recent example where secrecy can make data collection problematic for those attempting to reveal it. Computer security has now become a unique occupation all to itself. To be able to make computers secure, it is first necessary to know how to invade them. In some respects, the new computer security occupation is much like the police, in as much as they have to know criminals in order to access the criminal world. Computer security agents must also know how to hack into systems and in ways that are not detectable. A most recent best-selling nonfiction book describes how one very notorious computer hacker was able to access and steal what was thought to have been well-guarded data and move it about from one computer to another without being detected with "normal" equipment. When I first wrote about information assessment work almost thirty years ago, I made reference to a 1976 study edited by Arthur Bilke, entitled "Private Security: Standards and Goals from the Official Private Security Task Force Report." This document devoted only one and a half pages to computer fraud and never mentioned the need to have trained people to detect this phenomenon. Almost twenty years later, two nonfiction novels, *The Cuckoo's Egg* and *Takedown*, reveal that official surveillance scouts like the FBI and other law enforcement agencies are still not equipped to detect and uncover computer hackers, who really know what they are doing. I stated in my dissertation that I found this to be sociologically intriguing. Considering that twenty years have passed since that report, I find it even more intriguing.

Up to this point, the discussion has been to focus on overt scouts (workers in a variety of occupations and professions who seek out information). Seeing work from this perspective, we can begin to see how the line between "occupations" and "professions" can blur and make the distinction less meaningful. There is certainly nothing wrong with attempting to define what constitutes a "profession," but it is also helpful to be able to see work, all kinds of work, from perspectives that allow common elements and processes to emerge from professional and nonprofessional work alike. Work that can be classified as IA work includes both occupations and professions, so terms like *overt* and *covert scouts and sources* allow us to compare work across a variety of occupations and professions, which do not appear to have anything in common at first blush.

This has certainly been true of Everett Hughes' sociology. When we continue our logical extension of overt scouts, we come to the realization that some IA work must be conducted from a covert perspective. When sources of information become so elusive that overt methods preclude any effective information flow development, then covert-scouting techniques must be developed. Spying among nations, corporations, or even between spouses necessitates the creation of specialized occupations (usually around techniques/technology) that allows entry to restricted sources of information. Some of these can be quite formalized and institutionalized as in the case of the FBI and CIA within American society. It is difficult to study this kind of work for a variety of reasons. They generally don't want people poking around in their midst, asking about their work techniques. This is why we don't know much about espionage work apart from novels and a few "tell-all" books. Most of this literature comes to us from the Vietnam War days, particularly Marchetti and Marks' book, *CIA and the Cult of Intelligence*. We, as a society, have been told that the CIA has changed since the Cold War days. This remains to be seen since we are not permitted to observe the organization from any critical perspective. However, twenty years ago, Marchetti and Marks revealed the following:

> Counter espionage, like covert action, has become a career specialty in the CIA; some clandestine operators do no other type of work during their years with the agency. These specialists have developed their own clannish subculture within the Clandestine Services, and even other CIA operators often find them excessively secretive and deceptive. The function of the counter espionage officers is to question and verify every aspect of CIA operations; taking nothing at face value, they tend to see deceit everywhere. In an agency full of extremely mistrustful people, they are professional paranoids. (Marchetti and Marks, 1975, p. 213)

Most of our knowledge of covert scouts comes to us from the pages of novels—not only spy novels but from the genre of detective fiction as well. Probably the most common and well-known example of a covert scout is the ubiquitous PI—the private investigator made famous by both British and American authors, Hollywood movies, and dozens of television programs. It may be one occupation that everyone thinks they know by these various romanticized versions. The occupation is quite different in reality. The bulk of the work for most PIs is done for law firms or insurance companies or for dealing with divorce and child custody cases. The private investigator becomes a covert scout for hire. Much of this kind of work breaks down into the following categories: (1) injury claims on insurance companies to determine if physical activity coincides with the claimed injury, (2) preemployment background checks for companies needing trustworthy employees, (3) assessing the credibility of witnesses for legal cases, (4) working covertly within organizations to detect internal theft of property or information, (5) investigate fires, accidents, and damage within organizations, and (6) working in computer fraud. This does not paint a very glamorous picture of PI work. They do collect information that others attempt to conceal. They may have little else to do with this information once it is collected. They can put it into the information flow and let others assess it.

Before we move on to the monitoring phase of IA work, let me briefly summarize. In developing a flow of information, there are a variety of occupations that can be classified as scouts who encounter both willing and unwilling sources. Covert and overt scouts and sources have been explored. Developing a flow is only the beginning of the IA process. A host of other subprocesses is involved once the information faucet is turned on. We next will turn to the monitoring of information within organizations and see how the processes of advising, forecasting, and criticizing can become full-time jobs for occupations and professions alike.

Monitoring the Flow

One of the most obvious subprocesses in assessing information is monitoring at various points within an organization. This can be a very complex part of the IA process, for it can be broken into several components: observing, screening, interpreting, criticizing, and sorting. These can be further reduced, but only these will be discussed in this chapter.

Observing the Flow

Most work involves some form of observing information as it passes through an organization. Written and electronic information abounds in any organization. Those who observe this flow of information can be located at any point. Secretaries and clerks are in perfect positions to observe this flow. Screening and sorting this information may be the role of secretaries and clerks, but the more serious monitoring process usually takes place at the line or staff positions.

Screening the Flow

Since everyone in an organization is usually able to observe information at some point in their work, it is more important to understanding the screening process since it is much more specific. Physicians and lawyers screen information all the time. So do police and security personnel. Sometimes, this screening process can overlap and be difficult to sort out in terms of jurisdictional disputes (Abbott, 1988). Rubenstein's classic 1973 study, "City Police," illustrates what can happen to information just within a single police department:

> The patrolman's sector is not exclusively his, but what he learns on it is his own. His colleagues the wagon men and other patrolmen—cannot come into his sector for any reason without informing him, unless they want to risk his wrath. But others may penetrate his territory regularly without prior consultation. His sergeant and lieutenant do not have to tell him what they are doing, and an astute sector man often spends some of his time trying to find out what his superiors are doing in his sector. Plain clothes men, headquarters units and detectives may operate without his knowledge . . . Less frequently, but with great discretion, his sector is visited by agents from the district attorney's office, state police agents, military policemen seeking deserters, F.B.I. agents, federal treasury, narcotics and alcohol agents; insurance investigators and private detectives, too, operate without his knowledge. He has no control over any of these men, but he is usually not concerned about what they are doing unless he is involved in some kind of illicit or illegal actions. But his colleagues do

> interest him and he does have a measure of control over them. He fortifies his control by denying them the information he accumulates and sharing it with them only when he feels it is to his benefit. (Rubenstein, 1973, pp. 214-215)

It is not difficult to see the importance of screening from the above example. Screening can lead to withholding of information from others, from one organization to another, and from one nation to another. Here we see the classic example of Everett Hughes's concept of "dirty work" in action. Police are always in a position to establish contact with those in the criminal world. The police officer that gains information about a crime can relay the same information up the organization and be protected if it is revealed that the officer has become part of the criminal activity. If the officer chooses to screen such information so that they appear not to be detecting criminal activity, they may not have the organizational protection when they need it.

Screening can impact a larger audience, including an entire society. An example of this can be taken from the motion picture industry, particularly the occupation of movie censor. Movies do get screened prior to release, and this has taken place since 1907 when Chicago and New York City established ordinances, requiring police inspection and licensing of all movies to be shown to the general public (Randall, 1968, p. 11). Two years later, the first censorship court case emerged in Block v. Chicago, where the Illinois Supreme Court upheld the ordinance. The most significant case, however, was in 1915, when the U.S. Supreme Court ruled in the Mutual Film Corporation v. Ohio that movies were not free speech (Randall, 1968, p. 12). For the next thirty-seven years, prior censorship legislation occurred in most states and U.S. cities. Eventually, the prior restraint legislation led to the development of self-regulation within the movie industry and can be traced back to 1933 with the creation of the Film Board of National Organizations (ten groups in all) and whose costs the Motion Picture Association of America (MPAA) underwrote. The report of this censor team was called the "Green Sheet" and was an attempt to screen what the public would view.

All of this has lead to the current rating system that now prevails in the America film industry. Even though this system has been modified over the years, it is essentially in place as a guide to parents of moviegoers. One of the rare anthropological studies on this industry reveals some interesting aspects of screening:

> Like primitive man, Hollywood prefers magic to either fighting or reasoning with menacing forces. The forces of censorship seem to most Hollywood people so powerful and so unreasoning as to take on the quality of a black magician aiming malevolent spells. A set of taboos, while it does not destroy this threatening power, seems to the industry to ward it off, just as primitive man thinks magic and taboos lessen the dangers of the supernatural and the evil intentions of other beings. (Powdermaker, 1950, p. 56)

Let us move on to yet another occupation that screens information during the monitoring process. The journalist does not use all the information collected when submitting a story for publication. However, the main source of power to screen information within a news organization is the managing editor (Sieglman,1973, p. 135). It is from this desk that the news of the day is organized and formulated. Since the "important" news is selected for the front page, all story placements rest with this editor, for they are in almost total control over what goes to print as news. Leon Sigal maintains that page-one makeup illustrates most clearly how this screening process is played out:

> The managing editor calls on the national, foreign, and metropolitan editors to describe in brief the most important stories their desks will have for tomorrow's paper. The financial, culture, or even the sports editor may also offer a story or two from his desk as worthy of page one play. As each editor runs down his list, the others comment on the substance of the stories and raise issues of news gathering and makeup, suggesting new angles to check in writing the story and possible links to take into account in making up the paper. The managing editor then makes his selections for page one, relying almost exclusively upon the editors' lists, but once in a while glancing at the news budgets drawn up by the desks and asking editors about a story they did not mention. Discussion follows, some of it heated, as editors try to change his mind. The meeting breaks up after fifteen or twenty minutes, but the fight over page one may rage throughout the rest of the afternoon. (Sigal, 1973, p. 27)

It appears from Sigal's work that the larger the news organization, the greater the power it retains in screening out some information and allowing what remains to become printed as news. It appears that a newspaper editor is a perfect example of an occupation that screens information, many times to the great exasperation of the reporters. As a news organization grows larger and more complex, there are more people who are involved in the screening process.

The mass-produced quality of the news can have a tremendous impact on a society, especially when information is screened in such a way that no one really knows for sure who may be doing it. News production can lead, according to Johnstone, Slawski, and Bowman, to greater dependence upon large-scale organizations:

> We feel that the strain between the needs of formal organizations to regulate and control their functions and the need of the individual worker for autonomy is especially critical for journalism because of current trends in the organization of the news industry. Increasing centralization leads inevitably to greater bureaucratization, and this together with the introduction of computerized routines in the news room will further increase the necessity or coordination and control over news work. (Johnstone, et al., 1976, p. 185)

An example of a large bureaucratic news organization's impact on shaping the news comes from Gay Talese's delightful work:

> High power at the Times is a vaporous element where energy is harnessed, pressure is built, decisions emanate from a corporate collective, but it is difficult to see which man did what, and it often seems that nobody really did anything. Decisions appear to ooze out of a large clutch of executive bodies all jammed together, leaning against one another, shifting, sliding, shrugging, bending backwards, sideways and finally tending toward some tentative direction; but whose muscles were flexed? Whose weight was decisively felt? The reporters in the newsroom do not know. (Talese, 1978, p. 121)

Screening work examples can be developed from a variety of occupations and professions, but it is definitely one of the key kinds of work that gets performed and defines security work. People can be subject to security procedures that can be applied to specific spaces in order to control them. Those who pass through the gates can find security guards. The following description illustrates how this can work:

> Security operations attempt to normalize social interaction for purposes of control. The taken-for-granted rules that guide everyday discourse are replaced by rational procedures in order to objectify encounters between an agent and those he secures. Rules are established to dictate what is relevant about prospective entrant, and thereby to regulate territorial access with formalized criteria of membership, e.g., only persons with a pass will be permitted to enter. Guards are instructed to treat these criteria, e.g., passes, as evidence of legitimacy. The agent's focus on the evidence transforms his gaze into an act of power and renders the perspective entrant subordinate to rational guidelines which transcend this meeting: the latter must present the relevant information if he or she is to enter legitimately. (Altheide, 1975, pp. 181-190)

Using this description as the theoretical basis of security work, Altheide goes on to explain how the application of the rules differs according to the settings and situations between the securer and the secured. The main conclusion from this article is that security procedures are designed only to apprehend the amateur, the naive, and the stupid, while the professional is capable of using the knowledge of security procedures as a means of appearing "legitimate." Again, according to Altheide, " . . . presence implies acceptance according to the rules of security, and this makes us all vulnerable." (Altheide, p. 184)

Interpreting the Flow

After observing and screening the flow of information, there comes a time when someone must interpret what has been received. Sometimes, the observer and screener can also be the interpreter, and all of this can happen quite quickly. Individuals or individual groups, depending upon the work organization and the work itself, can perform at any one time each of these processes. Many occupations and professions are defined for their interpretive work even though they may observe and screen also. Certainly, law and medicine are defined in this manner. As more and more specialization takes place in both occupations and professions, so, too, does the interpretive process. William James has discussed two concepts that are applicable here. James makes the distinction between "acquaintance with" and "knowledge about."

Any organization that deals with information assessment requires occupations that have specific "knowledge about." The result has been the growth of specialized interpreters (or advisors) that serve a specific clientele, either outside or inside the organization. Many times, the knowledge is so specific that the interpreters can become the "experts." According to Guy Benveniste, this relationship can be compared to the "prince and the pundit," where the prince represents an individual or group and the pundit is the expert, "the man of knowledge or social architect." Benveniste bases his analogy upon the Machiavellian advisor but examines contemporary experts:

> Modern Princes governing modern technological societies do not dispose of experts as they wish. They cannot avoid expert advice because modern technological societies are vastly complex sets of interacting subunits, and no modern Prince can comprehend the complexities of his domain. A modern Prince is highly dependent on the quality and reliability of the information, advice, and guidance he receives. In fact, he may appear to be a prisoner in the hands of his advisors, the specialized experts in his retinue. (Benveniste, 1972, p. 3)

One aspect of this type of relationship that has pretty much remained constant throughout the centuries is the one-on-one relationship between an advisor and a client in the political arena. Herbert Goldhamer refers to the "solitary man" notion of a ruler as a cliché. He contends all rulers throughout history have had their interpreters of information, although in recent times, more interpreters must share the limited time their client is able to give to the one-on-one encounter:

> The advisor evokes the image of one placed close to the ruler, of one who, for the most part, communicates his advice orally. When, however, we review the various means

by which the ruler has, over the centuries, sought or received aid in his policy deliberations, this image is rapidly effected by a great many others—the ruler searching in dreams . . . the ruler and his advisors sifting the historian's treasurers for lessons in the art of statecraft; the young prince absorbing from a tutor lessons intended to serve him in the days of his research and policy institutes, that is, of an immense structure of institutionalized advisory services. Nor do these images by any means exhaust those that the history of the advisor can provide. (Goldhamer, 1978, p. 28)

Goldhamer continues by discussing that advice giving has changed from a verbal tradition to a written one. In this respect, we can see information boundaries forming around the IA work (Davis, 1985). This is why interpretive work generally comes in written form in medicine and law. Sometimes, however, information is observed and interpreted instantaneously. The gaming official in sports is one example of this kind of work. The gaming official is both the observer and interpreter. When researching this unique occupation, it was found that gaming officials do not call every infraction they see. There is generally a feeling among those who work as officials that detecting all fouls of play will not improve a sport since the fouls detected (according to Norm Schacter, a retired National Football League referee) "have little to do with the operation of the game or the actual play. You wouldn't call them because you're not out there to detect everything, you're out there to make sure no one gets an unfair advantage" (Lapin, 1977, p. 47).

The one sport, where the officials particularly feel this issue, is professional basketball. Since called infractions can result in the expulsion of a player from the game, there is added pressure on the officials calling a game since highly paid players (those who draw the most fans) may find themselves sitting out most of the games. Since basketball is one of the fastest games, the spectators pay to see the "fast action." The officials stand between the rules of the game and the economic realities of the owners. This is probably why Wilt Chamberlain was able to play fourteen years—1,045 games—without fouling out once. (Lapin, p. 50)

The sociological significance of interpreting information is profound, and further study of these kinds of occupations and professions may reveal to us a greater understanding between social control of information and what becomes knowledge in a society.

Criticizing the Quality of Information

In addition to the above three types of monitoring, there can occur, at least in some work, the need to assess the quality of information passing through or even making critical assessments of those doing the monitoring. This can result in the continuous process of checking the reliability of both the information and the methods used to collect it. This is certainly the case in medicine and most manufacturing organizations. Critical monitoring relates to what most consider being quality control and can be found to be both a formal type of work procedure (part of someone's regular task structure) or on an informal basis.

Formal critical monitoring can be exemplified by a variety of occupations found in a number of divergent work organizations. The following are two common forms that can be found in most organizations. Quality control personnel are located in many production line industries to criticize the quality of work up the line. Supervisors and managers are regularly called upon to conduct a critical appraisal upon the employees who work in their departments or divisions.

We can see from these two examples alone that various streams of information can be subjected to such critical monitoring. In the first example, we see that products become the source of information while the employees become the focus of another. In fact, most business organizations establish critical monitoring around these two—the products and the employees. The criteria used in the process are usually based upon some cost-benefit formula. The criteria of what gets "caught" in terms of product quality or employee performance can vary widely. Since the early 1970s, this subject has dominated the business literature, especially the differences between American standards of performance and those of European or Asian cultures.

Examples of critical monitoring are plentiful outside of business also. The fine arts are one area that has established a long history of critical monitoring. William Faulkner's delightful work on the studio musician was very graphic on this point, namely, the playing of even one sour note can lead to dismissal (Faulkner, 1971). This is critical monitoring at one extreme end of the continuum. We can see how specialized this type of monitoring can become when we focus on the performing arts. The most famous occupation of critical monitoring in this social world is, of course, the drama critic. William Rusher, a syndicated columnist and political commentator, points out the power of this particular occupation:

> No political columnist ever acquires (fortunately) the clout that is wielded by a major drama critic. I feel positively sorry for Richard Eder, the principal theatre critic of the New York Times. Through no fault of his, legitimate plays in America live or die, depending very largely upon how well they do on Broadway. And it just so happens that Eder's opinion concerning a new play is the most important single datum affecting that play's success on Broadway. The result is that hundreds of thousands of dollars, and hundreds of thousands of man years of hard work, and untold amounts of talent or even genius can be lavished upon a new play—and then vanish in a puff of smoke if Eder, after watching it once, says he didn't care for it. (Rusher, 1977, p. 35)

The drama critic is important sociologically, for this role becomes a regulator within the social world of performing arts. This particular occupation represents almost a pure form of critical work since the critic does have so much power in shaping the opinions of the audience. The delivery of formal criticism is also a common occurrence in a variety of fields, even though the drama critic may have the greatest power of them all. A movie critic also has some power, but the movie will not suffer as greatly from a negative review as does a play. A play can go away overnight with a negative review while a movie may play on and even become popular despite a poor review.

Critical monitoring in education is yet another example of critical work. According to Everett Hughes, teachers will describe their work from a variety of perspectives, but rarely will they call themselves a "grader of papers." For the most part, teachers are continually being critics of their students' performances and the information that they produce. In many respects, critical work plays a major role in the work of professional educators. This is also true of many other occupations and professions. Review boards, oversight committees, commissions, grand juries, judges, special prosecutors, accreditation teams, and thousands of other such organizations perform critical monitoring on a daily basis. As a form of work, it has not been adequately studied.

Another aspect that should also be studied is the way work gets informally criticized within organizations. It is certainly evident in medicine where subordinates and superordinates establish and maintain an elaborate system of informal criticism. Even Friedson's work has demonstrated that informal criticism is more likely to occur between physicians on a day-to-day basis. This can change if formal charges are instituted against another physician and formal review board forces physicians to a more formal process. Much of the interaction within teaching hospitals between the house physicians and the intern/residents has a great deal to do with this informal criticism. During the last fifteen years, many have taken advantage of this kind of informal criticism to establish innovative ways to bring this information into collective awareness so that organizational changes can take place. The business world has labeled this *quality circles*, *total quality management*, *re-engineering*, and a host of other terms, which relies heavily on informal critical monitoring.

Sorting

This is one of the last major components in the monitoring process. Sorting involves the prioritization of information so that it can be moved to the proper place within the organization. Not only can information be sorted but people may also since they may be the source of the information sought. Certainly, police and medical works move people about as routine since the person is the most likely source of information for both kinds of work.

It is really the sorting of paper and electronic files that makes up the bulk of this kind of work, and this does require extensive procedures in most organizations to perform this task. Sorting criterion is probably what makes up a vast amount of job descriptions in companies throughout the world. The sorting process can become more complex as the size of the organization increases. Knowing where to send information becomes part of the job description. This may require a solid knowledge of the organization and the various functions that comprise it. Since every organization has several streams of information running through it (external as well as internal: financial, managerial, technical, and other substantive kinds of information), those who sort information must learn how to move this information around.

This major process in IA work—sorting information and making sure the flow of information into, and through, an organization is constant and steady—can be divided up into three subprocesses: expanding the flow, shifting it, and stopping the flow altogether. Steadying the flow of information, insuring a predictable flow to various parts of the organization, will be our first focus.

Keeping a steady flow of information moving through an organization can be a key managerial function in most organizations. When information is not forthcoming from external sources, the flow must be expanded. Doctors need patients, and lawyers need clients, and both professions rely heavily on single sources of information. When patients and clients stop coming through the door hospitals, law firms can find themselves in financial trouble. The newspaper business relies heavily on multiple sources and can generate news by increasing reporters. Even reporters can find themselves relying too heavily on single sources and find themselves too dependent on these sources. They may, in fact, find themselves being used by their sources or find that their written work suffers by trying not to offend them. Editors have the option of using wire service stories in addition to their own reporters. Most editors of large urban dailies will usually choose their own staff reporters over the wire service, but many small papers really don't have this choice.

So many organizations find themselves with either too little or too much information to process that leads to the necessity to steady a flow once it begins. Doctors keep patients waiting, as do many other occupations and professions, who collect information from people and use that information to assess an outcome. So IA work can involve a great deal of shifting information from one part of the organization to another to insure that the right person gets to see it. Matching information with sources can be rather important in hospitals, medical clinics, law firms, welfare offices, police departments, and newspapers. Even the shifting of information around barriers in order to keep a flow going is also a possibility (see chapter three on work-arounds).

Finally, at some point, however, the flow of information must stop, and an assessment made. Those who collect information may be ordered not to accept any more, or they may make this decision on their own. The time between the cessation of information and an assessment may involve hours, weeks, or even months. Since there have been no studies, which can tell us what can happen between stopping the flow and the final assessment, we are left with speculation at this point.

Assessment of the information can occur in both verbal and written forms. These can be sequential where the workers take in information, make an assessment (which can remain verbal or placed in writing), and continue to collect information so that further assessing can occur. Certainly, medical work is like this. Making a diagnosis (both verbal and written assessments) and then administering an action based upon that assessment requires constant collection and monitoring of patient information. If the action is successful, then a medical problem may have been solved for a patient. Other written or verbal assessments may be one-event items, like IQ tests, SAT scores, and the like. These kinds of data may follow a person their entire life. Courts, especially those that make precedent setting decisions, can appear to make one-time assessments without the benefit of continuous monitoring of information.

Depending on the work being done, some information may remain within an organization rather than be dispersed outside of the organization. Many times, verbal information is retained within a knowledgeable circle with no written boundaries to consider. Other times, such as in journalism, the written form takes on a formal presentation in the normal distribution of the "news." Once in print, the information that once flowed through the editing process now becomes the news. It is yet another example of when verbal information takes on written form.

Lee Sigelman's study of twenty-five years ago, where he collected data on two daily newspapers in "Southeast City," discovered that newspapers are greatly influenced by their publisher. According to one of his informants, "Any newspaper, it seems with a single ownership . . . reflects the thinking of the publisher and his philosophy. To a great extent, the publisher *is* the newspaper and the newspaper *is* the publisher" (Sigelman, 1973, p. 135).

The impact of the publisher (monitor) upon the content of the news indicates to many researchers that the newspaper is part of the political institution of any society. Robert Park expressed the point in the following:

> It is true we have not studied the newspaper as a biologist
> has studied the potato bug. But the same may be said of every
> political institution, and the newspaper is a political institution

quite as much as Tammany Hall or the board of alderman are
political institutions. (Park, 1952, p. 103)

Much of the information that becomes a written document in
organizations may not appear in such dramatic fashion as in news and
medical or legal organizations. Most of the information that makes up the
flow within an organization consists of memos, reports of various kinds,
or just fill-in-the-blank forms. Some may be just electronic notations
that never get put onto paper such as e-mail but can still be filed away
within the organization. Information has a tendency to build up and
accumulate within organizations. Some can be retained in the form of
files, microfilm, and computer disks; while other reports can be released
as official information in the form of newspapers, news magazines,
books, journals, news releases, and a variety of other formats.

Whatever the final informational product is, it usually involves
the movement of information from a verbal state to a written form.
Information begins to take on official shape, where verbal flow can turn
into a written report. In the case of the reporter, the information can be
sold on the street. In the case of the physician, the official report is given
only verbally to the patient since the written report remains within the
domain of medicine (the hospital or clinic).

Chapter Six

The Urban Artist

This chapter was written for two reasons. I always wanted to write this paper with Anselm Strauss since he knew me as both a painter and sociologist. I painted his home in San Francisco, inside and out, and was a trusted craftsman for him and his wife Fran. I matched colors, never spilled a drop of paint, refinished their kitchen cabinets, and even gave them a plaque once, for surviving a remodeling project, which included the construction of a small bathroom on their sun deck. We talked about writing this paper on several occasions, but both of us were always busy with something, and we never did it. Some of the ideas in this are Anselm's, some my own, and the others are just a great deal of Hughes.

The second reason for writing this now has to do with recognizing the gifted house painters that give so much character and beauty to our urban environments, especially my beloved city of San Francisco. Since I helped make San Francisco a work of art, I want to acknowledge the man who taught me how to be an urban artist, Mr. Emil Zollinger, now a retired artist/contractor, who still resides in "The City" with his wife Caroline.

No one ever called us artists, not even within our own social world of painting. Nor did our work attract the attention of the art world. We did get some recognition as a group, at least in San Francisco, when a book appeared under the title of *Painted Ladies*. This was a book on Victorian architecture in San Francisco that illustrated the various combinations of colors that such a house could sustain. Several of our jobs were displayed but without the recognition by the author that we had done them. It was usually the color consultant who was recognized in the book, and this was usually Bob Buckner, a local German painter, who moved into the consulting business during the 1970s and became famous in the 1980s.

There were several aspects to this process of claiming the work as art even though it was never verbalized. The first process in all of this is identifying "the job" as art and distinguishing it from the other jobs, which a painter can find themselves doing in an average painting season. The next process is claiming the job as property. Most of the time, "the job" was defined as art if the work took place on a Victorian house, especially if the owner was willing to pay the price of having four or more colors applied. It was usually the number of colors that defined "the job" as art, but there was even some debate about this. Our crew painted numerous Victorians, and I believe we viewed them as special each time, even if we used only two to three colors. Three colors was generally the minimum on a Victorian since everyone wanted a contrast between the sash and the window frame, and then the body of the house would generally be different. At other times, there could be from five to six colors applied in such a manner as to accent the gingerbread, which defines the Victorian style. Eight colors were a stretch even though the *Painted Ladies* contain several who made this stretch. There was never a doubt when we did such work that we looked upon ourselves as artists. This was especially evident when the contrast between the start and the finished product was so great. Many Victorian houses in San Francisco had been neglected to the point of being classified as seedy. Some houses had their last paint job before World War II, and the degree of disrepair was evident. It was this kind of job that we viewed as our property and became a challenge to our craftsmanship.

The last process to this kind of work, which made me see that we were really artists, is the visibility of the work itself. The work of many trades is hidden and out of sight of the public view. Plumbing and electrical work is generally this way; at least the bulk of what they do is intentionally hidden behind walls, floors, and ceilings, not so with carpentry and painting. These are the visible trades along with the glaziers, gutter specialists working with copper, and roofers. This is why it was easy to claim the job as our property since it was always out in the open and visible to anyone driving on the street or walking by. It even occurred to me at times that we should be signing the corner of the house just before we drove away for the last time. This would have seemed pretentious to Emil, but I know he took pride in all of the Victorian jobs we completed. From 1973 to when I last painted for him in the summer of 1990, Emil and "the crew" must have worked on at least thirty-five Victorians in San Francisco. Considering that there are only about 350 such structures remaining in "The City," this is a remarkable accomplishment for a painting contractor with only five painters on his crew at the peak of any painting season.

The Urban Artist

Anselm would have approached this topic from a social psychological perspective, and I will try to do the same. The main focus should be the relationship between the home owner/client and the painting contractor/artist. The fine line is between what the client demands and what the contractor "recommends" in terms of color selection and preparation prior to final coat. On the one hand, the artist/contractor must be able to "read" the client in such a way as to provide the best public display of taste for the client, similar to what clothes do for an individual.[50] This paper will reflect my experiences on one urban artist crew in San Francisco, and although I had many months of observations, I was never able to learn the artist/contractor's technique of how he did this. I believe much of what he did was to ensure the client that the finished product (a painted home) would reflect very positively on the home owner not only to their neighbors but also to the general public who may drive or walk by.

The more autonomy the contractor demands in this regard, the more artistic power he has in the client—contractor relationship. The artist/contractor will want to convey the best public expression of taste for their client (similar to what Goffman has called their "social identity,") as well as capturing their personal one as well[51]. In addition to conveying a public display of client taste, the artist/contractor must also take into consideration the taste of the immediate audience as well—the client's neighbors. It is this kind of artistic negotiating that contributes to the success of the artist/contractor.

In addition to the artistic aspects of the work, the artist/contractor must also be concerned with the technical/labor perspective and the temporal factors that can be negotiated with the client. Again, I believe Anselm would have insisted that this paper reflect the negotiation of temporal issues with respect to any particular painting job. Since the job is priced on the basis of time spent at the site, it is critical that enough time be allocated to insure a quality product. A client cannot request a quality finish without paying for quality preparation. The artist/contractor will not allow one without the other—a major criterion for establishing a distinction between a regular painting contractor and the artist/contractor. Once the client has agreed to what the artist/contractor recommends, the technical/labor phase can begin. In the painting business, this would just be called "working the crew" since it is the crew who performs the technical labor. This paper will describe how the urban artists work not only with their clients but also with their crews.

There are certain occupational traditions that dictate how work gets performed in art worlds[52], and the urban artist is no exception. One of those conventions involves autonomy over temporal contingencies—a factor that allows the artist/contractor to set the pace of his own work. One way of doing this is to have several jobs going at the same time so the waiting time of the crew can be minimized. The job must become the property of the artist/contractor. The job as property has been the theme of others[53] (especially his discussion of capturing). The paint job can be captured in a number of ways prior to the actual starting time. Since the temporal aspects of work involve both scheduling and work rhythms, it is important to understand the distinction as it relates to the painting trade.

Scheduling Jobs

The scheduling of jobs can be categorized as interior or exterior. The bulk of exterior jobs are scheduled and completed during the best weather months, and the interiors are usually saved for the wintertime. Of course, in California, and San Francisco in particular, this aspect of the work does not follow any ridged pattern other than a knowledge that rain is more prevalent from January through April. Fog is another predictable period (June-August), but it is never foggy all the time during the summer, and high fog causes little problems anyway. It is the low, heavy fog that can cling to surfaces and keep them damp, which can cause the problems. So even during the best of weather, a painter will always try to have interior jobs as backup to keep his crew busy even if the unexpected weather is realized.

So the precise scheduling of a building (from start to finish) can only be approximate unless the owner is willing to pay extra for this service. Most owners are willing to pay the regular rates and hope for the best.

Since the scheduling is difficult to predict, it becomes necessary to buy time and set up the falls or scaffolding in order to capture the job. This is similar to what Glaser calls "elsewhereism" with respect to subcontractors of any kind. Once the job has been captured, a number of days can pass before the painters feel obligated to go back and start the preparation work. Since the "prep" work can be 75 percent of the job, it is necessary to do this as quickly as possible since a painting crew can bog down in this extremely physical and dirty work. This is why the foreman position is so difficult since they must set the pace of the work for the others.

Pacing is everything in the painting business since several jobs are always waiting once one is completed. Keeping a rapid pace in the "prep" work can buy a little time for the painters once they start the finish coat. Since this is the time allowed as "artist work," it shouldn't be rushed.

As a member of the crew, we could never tell how much time we had on any of the jobs, only that the pace had to be brisk at any time. Generally, we could get a feel if we were ahead of schedule by subtle cues from Emil. If he were relaxed at the end of the day, or if he bought beer and we drank one after work, we could generally agree that things were going well and that the artistic work would be relaxed. Again, *relaxed* is a relative term since we were always keyed up around the boss and never appeared to be relaxed in any sense. This was part of his European training that was passed down to us. In many respects, we were always "at school" with Emil, a school with walls, but we had better be doing something with those walls at all times: preparation, priming, caulking, or finish coat.

Working the Crew

There was never a break in the work once we started at seven thirty. At noon, we would break for half an hour and eat lunch, but we always ate together and never allowed to wander off on our own. It was a strict socialization process that made us all very close in the end. Those that smoked could only smoke at lunch time or after everything was cleaned up and put away at 4:00 p.m. On Fridays, we would sometimes meet for a beer after work, where Emil would become another person. The master painter would be the relaxed Emil until we would arrive again on Monday morning and start the process once again.

One always had to be alert to his "lessons" since we never knew when he would allow us to watch. Talking with others over the years who worked apprenticeships in a variety of work (photographers, sculptures, stage directors, and motion picture camera operators as examples), the ability of picking up various techniques is time consuming and gained by doing the work and observing those who have mastered the craft. Those who may enjoy their teaching role give some things (techniques, solutions to various problems confronted on the job, or pacing of work for example) away quite freely. However, there does come a time when the master begins to see the apprentice as a potential competitor and won't contribute any more information. Even asking questions will result in some kind of stonewalling. Mixing colors in the painting trade is one of these techniques that are not freely given. It is, therefore, one of the more difficult aspects of learning the craft of painting. It was defining these times as "artist times," which defines the theme of this paper.

Emil would never verbalize when we were getting the lessons. We had to watch the process as part of the work. If we were doing something close to the portable "shop" (usually defined by where all of the equipment was set out on a drop cloth), then we could watch the mixing of colors. Matching colors was more interesting and complicated, for it involved taking a paint with the proper base and applying the various pigments to a point where it was close enough to do a wet sample if he were matching to an existing can of paint or a dry sample if he were matching an existing surface.

Wet sampling was done by taking the putty knife and dipping it into the paint to be matched and then directly dipping it into the newly mixed paint. One can tell if the new color is getting close. One tries to have a lighter first match so one can add additional color to move it to the exact color. When the original paint and the new paint cannot be distinguished on the putty knife, then the new paint can be used for the job. Emil's matching jobs were so good that one could keep painting the same wall with the new color, but we always used a break in the building (a new wall, for example) to start the new batch.

Over the course of several years, one could attempt the matching process but only on your own time and your own jobs. Many of the crew would take paint jobs on weekends. We would always keep this information to ourselves since Emil would think that we were about to leave him and start our own business. I'm sure it happened to him many times over the years, and he wanted his crews loyal to him. However, since we were never allowed to do any of the matching, we never really knew how we stood as painters.

Wood graining and gold leafing were two parts of the artist formula we rarely saw. His graining jobs were mostly with European customers. He showed me the control panel piece he had done for someone with a small airplane. He had turned an aluminum panel into an oak panel. It was so good that one had to hold it to believe it. Special graining brushes were used to make the effect of oak wood grain, and the colors were perfect. Never was the wood grain lesson ever shown to me. The same was true of gold leaf. He described it in some detail, but he never showed me his method. Part of this was the fact that I was never really part of the profession of artists. I moved in and out too much for Emil to make me his heir to the business. If I would have remained with him throughout his career, I believe I would have learned it all.

We all had to be content to learn whatever we could in the time we had. The younger painters would come and go, and the older ones could not take the pace of his work. In any event, we became some of the best painters in the profession, and it was only after I had moved on to academia and painted only sporadically, for myself, or for other contractors, did I realize how much I had learned and how fast and accurate I had become. I could have been a real urban artist, but now I must be content with the knowledge that I had the pleasure of studying with one.

Job Knowledge

I have touched upon the more artistic qualities that urban artists can achieve, but there is still a great deal of general knowledge a painter must know before being competent. Painting is generally divided up on the types of surfaces one usually works. Industrial painters work mostly in metals; commercial painters do a great deal of interior work, and restorative painters work mostly with people's homes, both inside and out.

So the knowledge that a painter needs to understand restorative work is learning about the various surfaces in the area. In San Francisco, for example, many of the structures have been constructed of redwood, being built over one hundred years ago. Redwood was a common construction material in northern California, and San Francisco was a city with enough money to afford such construction. Redwood is a very soft material, and preparing it the wrong way can cause some major damage to the wood siding. Many of the inexperienced painters learned this lesson the hard way. Many times, the damage could never be hidden without replacing the siding itself. This knowledge of how to prepare wood was a major part of becoming a professional painter. Knowing how to finish off the job was part of becoming an urban artist.

Emil had selected restorative painting as his specialty. We could paint any home in San Francisco as long as it wasn't close to commercial property. Emil had been forced at one time to employ union painters—a period in his life he deeply resented. Union painters had to have breaks in the morning and the afternoon as part of the deal. They also established their own pace of work—something Emil could never understand since he should have been the one to do this. The union also had access to his books and his profit margins. This is what drove him to distraction. I really wasn't there during this period of his career, but I would hear stories about it years later.

After he was able to rid himself of the painters' union, he learned quickly that the union would not bother him if he remained in the household end of the business. The union was content to control the commercial work, and the others were happy to accept one piece of the pie. At one point in the 1960s, the painters' union had so many internal problems that major conflict finally erupted and culminated in a homicide within the union itself. I believe the union/nonunion battles have been a San Francisco tradition in all kinds of work—bartenders, chefs, and hotel employees. The history of the painters' union changed the way the work became divided in San Francisco, and Emil was a direct product of that battle.

Since Emil specialized in wood-framed structures, it was pretty sure he would begin to dominate the Victorian business once gentrification became a reality in San Francisco real estate. Families who had once lived in such homes began to sell them off or divided them up as apartments. The old owners wanted more modern homes outside of San Francisco, and for a period of time, the Victorian was viewed as old fashion. It wasn't until the 1960s when a new generation began buying them up and painting them in multiple colors. By the 1970s, everyone was looking for a Victorian to buy and restore. Emil was able to get a great many of these jobs since his work was so exact, and the finished product looked so elegant. We became Victorian specialists, and our artistry had a new audience.

Breaking Down the Work

After capturing the job, we could move into the preparation work. On wooden structures almost a hundred years old, you could expect to encounter over twelve coats of paint—many of the layers were lead based and tight to the wood. We generally began by burning off all the old paint from all surfaces by using hand-held butane torches. Believe me, holding a tank of butane all day can cause cramps in your hand, and we had plenty of them.

It was quite the art to burn an entire exterior. One had to learn how long to keep the flame on the paint before scraping it off with special tools. Only three or four layers of paint could be removed at any one torching since a flame could rise from the material quickly. Burning was the art of softening the old paint long enough to scrape it, and then we would apply the heat once again until we reached the wood itself. We could literally be burning off eighty to one hundred years of paint, and the fumes would remind us that much of it was lead based. The best time to burn was when it was a little damp, and the threat of fire was low. I was responsible for a five-alarm fire in San Francisco once, and I never wanted to go through that again. There was smoke damage to two apartments and some water damage to three others, but it was nothing really serious. Having to tell Emil what I had done was one of the most difficult tasks of my life. I still believe to this day that that experience changed my outlook on life. I had to accept responsibility for something that was my fault. I did it and lived to tell about it. If you knew Emil, you would be quite impressed with me right now.

But let me complete my description of the burning process. Since the heat of the flame would dull the blades, we could take breaks to sharpen them once again with a file. Sometimes, the five or six of us could spend a week just burning off the paint. The last fifteen minutes were spent sweeping up the dry paint chips and making it look like the paint came off by itself. No one would have known we had spent all day, dropping burned paint chips around the house. Not even a gum wrapper was left on the ground when we finished. This was in great contrast to many of the other painters in San Francisco, who left behind a considerable mess at the end of the day. Being neat was part of being an artist, and we learned early to keep it neat.

Following the burning of the paint, we would hand sand the various surfaces with #36 sandpaper and continue with the scrappers to obtain clean edges on all the surfaces. We used cloth gloves at all stages of the painting process, and with #36 paper, one could expect to go through several pair with hand sanding. Dust masks were a must for everyone but Emil, who didn't believe in them. I should mention here a clear demarcation between "clean" and "dirty" work from an urban artist's perspective.

Generally, all exterior work (up until the final coat) is dirty work, which is the bulk of each job. The final coat is the clean artistic portion of exterior work. On the other hand, almost all interior work is considered clean and desirable, especially for the older painters who don't have the stamina to perform exterior work. Of course, there are exceptions to this, but the concepts of what is clean and what is dirty are part of who gets defined as an urban artist. One could not continually do dirty work and be classified as an artist.

Another three to four days of this would be enough to prepare the building for the first primer coat. It was at this point when we would begin to anticipate what the final results would produce. Prior to putting the paint on the building, we would have to dust everything down once again and then apply the primer Emil had mixed. He would use a good exterior wood primer and then thin it with the paint thinner we had used to clean the brushes after each day. We never threw out any paint thinner. We would recycle it from its first use as the final rise of our brushes to its use as a paint thinner. Let me explain this in greater detail at the end under "End of the Day."

The primer coat, or coats, was applied quickly since it was all one color (off-white) and easy to work with since it was so thin. We would have to wait several days prior to caulking all the cracks, replacing the glaze around the windows, and generally getting clean lines ready for the finish coat. On the very best jobs, we would put another undercoat over all the caulk and putty (glaze) and then let that sit for a few days prior to the finish coat.

Upon returning for the finish coat, we would clean all the windows for a day and dust every thing down once again. This was the final day or two of preparation, and we would watch Emil get the final coat colors ready. He would put various samples of the colors on the lower part of the building so we could see how the colors contrasted and complimented each other. The home owners would either nod their approval or spend more time selecting various shades. All of this was the prelude to our final chapter for the crew. We would soon become the urban artists when we received our color buckets prepared by Emil.

The Final Coat

As I stated earlier, preparation of the house for the final coat is at least 75-80 percent of any paint job. The final coat is really the neatest and easiest portion of the job and is the portion that defines the artistic aspect of the work. All the surfaces have been dusted, the windows have been cleaned with razor blades and clean rags, and all the edges have been prepared so the paint will leave clean "lines." Lines are defined as the separation of one surface to another. The window sash is separate from the frame.

There can be various colors applied to the frame of a window but generally the sash (the portion of the window that holds the glass) is painted one color, which is distinct from the rest of the house. The contrast between the sash and the frame can be quite impressive. Since many Victorian homes have many windows, the color selected for the sash can make or break a painting job.

It was imperative to have a great contrast between the two surfaces. In many cases, we usually painted a minimum of three colors on the final coat. Most of the time, we were able to find a fourth color that highlighted a particular feature on the house that would give the final impression of "something special." On some jobs though, we were able to paint with five or six different colors, and contrasting result was quite impressive.

All paint jobs begin at the top of anything—a wall, a ceiling, a cabinet, and a house. Since most of our best jobs were scaffold professionally (we didn't do it ourselves and it was all secured to the building with strong wire), we didn't spend our artist time moving ladders. We moved from one level of the house to another with several buckets of different paint and finished our creation. The "body" color was defined as the color that was applied to all surfaces, not part of the window frames, the moldings, the gingerbread, the overhangs, the sash, the railings, the doors, and steps. Many times, the body color was applied by only one of us. This was done so the body color could have time to set up before another color was applied next to it.

Emil always used the highest, glossed exterior paint on his best jobs since it was more difficult to apply, but it would always wear the best of all paints. High gloss paint was always oil when we painted, but I understand that the air quality standards are such that only water-based paint is now allowed in the San Francisco bay area.

End of Day

Our day always began at seven thirty, and lunch was always at twelve. Since we always ate together and talked together, we were always working right up to 4:00 p.m. The end of the day was always welcomed since the pace of the work was so demanding, and we were never allowed to sit except for lunch. If we worked on scaffolding, we were still not permitted to sit while working, no matter what we were doing. We did so, of course, if Emil was not around, but we certainly never attempted it while he was on the job. He always insisted that sitting was a sign of laziness and was not what professional painters should be doing. So if we started at seven thirty and worked until twelve, we were on our feet without a break for four and a half hours. This made the afternoon more bearable since we were back at the job at twelve thirty for at least another three hours and fifteen minutes.

It was the last fifteen minutes where we prepared the brushes for storage and cleaned up our mess around the house. Cleaning the brushes was something that we did every day and in a manner that permitted us not to waste any thinner. Most of the time, we would use the first five-gallon bucket that contained the dirtiest thinner to get the initial paint out of the heel. The second bucket was a little cleaner, and we would wash the brush again using a steel brush to work out the dried paint. Then we would use the last bucket to do the finer cleaning. After this, we would replace the paper wrappers over the brushes and set them in clean thinner to soak. So when Emil needed paint thinner to thin primer, he would use the dirtiest thinner and then made the second bucket dirty; the "clean" thinner became the second, and we would use clean thinner to start the third bucket. The entire season would be handled this way, and we never needed to dispose of it.

While someone cleaned the brushes, others folded all the drop clothes and secured the ladders, and finally we cleaned ourselves up, and we did all of this in fifteen minutes. After the shop was secure, we changed clothes. We were always encouraged to arrive at work in casual street clothes and change into our painting gear on the job. We usually did this in a garage, but sometimes, we ended up behind a bush or car depending on the circumstances. Emil made us do this for several reasons. We looked neat and clean if we had to walk through the client's house prior to or after the workday. We could never carry paint on to another surface, like car seats or even furniture. We looked professional when we arrived, and we looked the same when we left the job (this is part of the "clean" vs. the "dirty" work discussed above). It also made it easier to walk into a store after work without looking soiled. This was all part of our professional training, and we found that most painters lacked this kind of style. In fact, we began to notice how offended we became when we would encounter painters in their work clothes in the supermarket or even on the streets. We became socialized to this practice.

It was also important to distinguish between what we wore on an exterior job and what was permitted on an interior. We kept the cleanest work clothes for the interior work, looking more like hospital orderlies than house painters. We were able to recycle our clothes this way by moving out the most soiled clothes (usually used for the burning, sanding, and priming) when we bought new clothes for an interior job. This way, we could have several changes of work clothes in our cases when we arrived or left at the end of the day.

We usually tried to gauge how we were doing during this time. We could tell if we were on schedule, or even ahead, by Emil's mood during the last fifteen minutes. On Fridays, we could expect a beer if the job was really difficult or even be treated to a pub beer if things went very well. I don't think Emil ever noticed that he was doing this, but it became obvious to the crew. We could relax and enjoy the beer and see a different part of Emil at the end of the day. Emil's work persona was quite different from his personal one, and we became quite good at reading this.

It was to our advantage to keep him happy, and working hard and steady was to guarantee this. I really think this was part of becoming an urban artist, and it was an experience that only a European trained artist/ contractor could provide. I had worked for other American contractors before, and there was nothing of the intensity or the artistry compared to Emil's approach to training his painters. I was witness to several painters who tried to become part of our crew and who were asked to leave at lunchtime because they weren't performing to Emil's satisfaction. Some were too slow, some tried to smoke while working, some sat down while working, and some just left after being reprimanded for one or more of the above infractions. After working for Emil, we were able to judge for ourselves who would make the cut and who wouldn't.

So the end of the day was a time to assess how we were doing and what to expect for the pace of work the next day. Since Friday was always payday, we were especially hard workers and looked forward to the end of that day. Making $12 per hour in 1974 was very good money, more money than some of my colleagues who were already teaching at university were making. So we always looked forward to Friday every week and to the end of the day, every day. We knew we were urban artists even though we never talked about it. We were Emil's crew, trained in a European manner to become some of the fastest, cleanest, and talented painters in San Francisco.

Chapter Seven

Administration as Fieldwork

This was written when I served as area director for an Overseas American University (OAU) in Asia from 1990-1998. The paper was initially written with the title "Managing Academic Labor: Reflections from the Middle." At the time, we had just introduced a new faculty development program within the Asian Division. We were debating among ourselves the impact of empowering the faculty with a faculty-driven program. Overseas American University has been providing undergraduate education to service members and their families in Asia since 1956.

As a sociologist, and an academic administrator, I feel that I have a license to address organizational issues, which impact upon the kind of work I do—managing academic labor within a university system.

There has been a long history of suspicion and jurisdictional challenges between those whose work is scholarship and teaching and those who manage them—the academic administrators. There have been a variety of reform movements over the years to make scholars accountable for the work they perform within a university setting. The most recent (the 1960s) has gone beyond American universities, and we can see changes occurring all over the globe. This reform movement has begun to reshape the jurisdictional disputes between the academic profession and those organizational changes, which force the accountability of public funds for higher education. Certainly not all of the changes that have occurred have been negative, but the changes represent a successful challenge to professional academic jurisdiction, which is still unfolding. The end result of this public accountability has been a transformation of the academic organization.[1]

Let me begin this discussion with some historical data that may give perspective to the jurisdictional dispute I refer to above. Hofstadter and Smith in American Higher Education quote Frederick A. P. Barnard, who wrote his memoirs in 1856:

> Gentlemen . . . you have undertaken the construction of a railway to connect the town of Jackson, Mississippi, with the town of Jackson, Tennessee. You have employed a corps of engineers. You have fixed the termini of your road and the general line of its course; but do you attempt to prescribe the details of the work of construction? You do not undertake to tell the engineers how they shall cross the river, or build that embankment, or cut that hill; that is the engineer's business. You employ engineers because they understand that business better than you. If you let them alone, they will do it judiciously. If you were to follow them mile-by-mile and compel them to make bridges and embankments and tunnels according to your ideas, the work would probably be spoiled. Just so in the University. You have asked us to educate the young men of Mississippi; you have appointed us because we are professional teachers and you believe we understand our business; you have prescribed the broad outlines of our work, and we have undertaken to do the work on those lines. Now, if you are to direct the details of the work at every step, you will succeed no better than you would succeed if you were to direct the engineers of the Mississippi Central in the same way. Our professional knowledge and experience will be set aside and rendered useless, and our whole work will probably be badly botched.[2]

Even though this problem has been part of the academic profession as long as the work has been part of the university, it does not mean that the problem is identified in the same manner. All societies have been influenced by the newly emerging business structure that has shaped many of the organizations in today's world; therefore, it is not difficult to see how the business structure has been superimposed over the old university organization of the past. The new reform movement has forced today's universities into a model of Weber's bureaucratic efficiency, a form now described by George Ritzer as the McDonaldization of society.

This has produced a unique blend of business management practices to be placed over the preexisting department-centered management structure that still prevails in most universities. During the last twenty years, universities have been pressured to replace the old department-centered structure with the new and "improved" business management practices of the CEO, line and staff configuration, and the need to control those who do the work—the academicians. There is a greater emphasis on standardizing tasks, auditing the time of the academics, and making sure what they do is "productive" and profitable according to those who are in positions to manage academic labor.

The end result of this organizational transformation is greater bureaucratic scrutiny. The student becomes a customer, the dean a line manager, and the courses and degree programs become the products that can be marketed and sold to the general public. Humanities courses that continually fail to attract students are in jeopardy of being replaced by business courses. All of this has led to greater scrutiny of those who represent the academic profession and practice the craft of teaching—the faculty. Just as Barnard describes above, the faculty are having greater difficulty in securing their professional role in the new business of knowledge production that has traditionally been within the jurisdiction of the university. The faculty have always defined the academic profession in the past, yet this new bureaucratic alignment is forcing a different perspective of who defines the profession. Those who manage academic labor have never defined the profession nor have those who benefit from their knowledge—the student—defined it. Yet we are beginning to see a significant shift away from how the profession was previously shaped.

When the student becomes part of the critical process to the point where he/she views the classroom process as a product, then the student also becomes part of the bureaucratic scrutiny and can define what is "good" or "bad" either intellectually or pedagogically.

Students have begun to challenge who should or should not be part of a university faculty. Courses, therefore, can be repackaged and presented differently if the buyer is not satisfied. This is the ultimate dilemma of creating the climate of public scrutiny of higher education. Again, let me reiterate that those who did the teaching and scholarship have traditionally defined the profession of university teaching. So those who defined the scope of the work have been replaced by those who now manage the work or are "customers" of the information. Historically, academics have relied upon the opinions of their peers and have not traditionally been fond of any kind of bureaucratic scrutiny. All intellectual action has always been opposed to "outside" interference, either by the administration, student, or general public.

This is why the change is so dramatic. If the one doing the teaching and scholarship is no longer defining the profession, then the profession itself may be in jeopardy. Although academic administrators manage faculty (and give the student/customer greater voice in determining the quality of the final product), administrators are not necessarily the definers of the academic profession. In the field of medicine, for instance, hospital administrators are no longer medical people. They may manage physicians, but the work of medicine is still defined by the doctors. Yet greater scrutiny of medical work during the last twenty years has eroded the physicians' jurisdiction as well.

The more we remove the faculty from the process of administration, the greater the risk of diminishing the profession itself. Academic administrators become aware of their role in increasing greater scrutiny of faculty if they have to insure that "quality" is being defined and that "product" and "customer" can be identified and managed. We may be demonstrating greater control over our academic labor, but we may be weakening a profession in the process.

OAU and Public Scrutiny

This entire process becomes even more of a concern for OAU and its European and Asian divisions since the military becomes part of the scrutiny process. The military becomes another "customer" who may regulate the way academic labor may be measured. Since we must continually "demonstrate" efficiency of our operations to those who can continually scrutinize every aspect of what we do as academic laborers, and as managers of that labor, it makes OAU even more vulnerable. In many respects, we may have become a hybrid organization of the military and not the autonomous institution we think we are.

We may have encouraged even broader powers of public scrutiny by allowing the contract, which regulates the relationship between the military and OAU, to determine what is and is not appropriate academic labor. We are continually fighting over our academic jurisdiction of what is ours (within the academic profession) and what is theirs (the military). Since the military becomes another layer of "customer," those in middle management positions on the OAU side (deans/area directors) find it very difficult to define their work from an academic standpoint.

There is little to distinguish an area director from a temp agency manager. Scheduling faculty to teach at various sites, making sure the "customer" (the education service officer within the military structure) is satisfied with the "personnel" (OAU faculty) assigned to a specific base, and insuring that the "classroom customer" (the student) is satisfied with the instructors' teaching methods are all part of the daily activities of the area directors. Such could be said of the managers of any temp agency.

If middle management (to use the terms of the new university structure where efficiency and accountability of faculty labor are more important than intellectual debate of scholarship) cannot be defined by their relationship to academic work, but rather with scheduling and customer relations, then the academic jurisdiction becomes blurred since the military is the one defining the terms of the relationship. The same can be said of any university that uses academic management in this manner to please a nonacademic audience. The irony of all of this is our inability as administrators to identify with the faculty who are the core of the academic profession. More administrative time is spent on better ways to measure faculty productivity than on how to incorporate the better aspects of the old academic structure to insure professional knowledge and experience are still defined by those who practice the craft of teaching.

There does appear to be one area where all of this jurisdictional dispute can be observed with greater clarity, and it may be an important indicator of whether academic or military criterion takes an upper hand in the delicate balance between the business of military education and the OAU system. This one area has been defined as "faculty development" and is part of the academy's reaction to the imposition of the business model of academic labor. Faculty development has become more of a movement to improve faculty performance by the faculty than to impose performance from above in a traditional business fashion (top-down-driven management practices). This movement has taken over twenty years to establish itself as a viable alternative to the new pressures from outside of the academy. For those in the OAU structure, it remains to be seen whether or not the military will "buy" this new faculty-driven program to improve what outsiders consider being "classroom productivity" and how faculty define the craft of teaching and scholarship.

The military will be the definers of whether or not the new faculty development program now being formulated within the OAU Asian Division will be an allowable expense (meaning that all moneys spent on this endeavor can be reclaimed from tuition). Although faculty development lies directly within the academic domain, its success or failure will ultimately be determined by outside forces. This is the crux of the jurisdictional dispute between public scrutiny and academic freedom.

Pressures outside of the OAU system or even outside of the academy itself may determine the success or failure of faculty development. All of this is just a current reminder of a process, which has been unfolding throughout the world of higher education. We must be ready to defend our academic jurisdiction with those who can demand greater scrutiny of us all.

We must keep in mind that our faculty can help us define our jurisdictional claims and that anything we can do to support their professional work we should do so. Just merely controlling the faculty (either from without or within) does not make us professional managers. We must begin to see that the roots of our profession lie at the very work of our faculty—the craft of teaching. If our efforts in the area of faculty development are thwarted by outside forces, we will lose important jurisdictional ground within our academic profession. If we allow this to happen, we become partly responsible for our own demise. We have a choice, and to me, the choice is clear.

Chapter Eight

Illusion Construction in American Culture

To discuss illusions as a social product is hardly new. George Herbert Mead, in discussing the concept of time, refers to the illusion building process as it relates to the past. David Maines, Noreen Sugre, and Michael Katovich have heeded Anselm Strauss's advice and explored the sociological significance of Mead's contribution to the concept of illusion building within an interactionist perspective.

> Thus, we can envision the use of mythical pasts as introducing the element of deception and trickery into Mead's political theory. It is entirely consistent with Mead's ontology (1936:335-336) to suggest that the world of illusion should be included in the structure of society. People create illusions and then induce others to impute meaning to them and act in accordance with those meanings. Illusions, however, must fit into the patches of empirical reality in order to be accepted as part of that reality. That is, in some measure they must be taken as real, validated, and incorporated into ongoing patterns of organization which constitute the social context of action. This process directs attention to the strategic employment of appearance (Lyman and Scott, 1970) and this Mead comes closer than previously thought the Machiavellian necessity of manipulation in the maintenance of social and political order. (Maines, et al., 1983, p.170)

Barry Schwartz's work on collective memory is also applicable. Schwartz states (1991, p. 221) that "Washington's post-Civil War transformation adds weight to Mead's and Halbwach's belief that the past is mutable, made and remade for present use."

I basically see two ways that illusion construction can take place within any society. The first is quite overt and involves a great many efforts on the part of various occupations and professions to construct an initial illusion that those within the culture accept as such. Novels, movies, plays, and entertainment in general would fall into this major category of illusion making. Covert illusions are much more complicated even though they may be even more prolific within any given society. It is the purpose of this paper to discuss both overt and covert illusions since they both play a significant role in all societies. I begin with one of the most obvious forms of illusion making in American culture today—Disneyland—and end with a discussion of how and why we construct illusions in covert ways. I use Disneyland, for I see it as a mirror that reflects American culture, and it becomes a perfect metaphor to describe how public illusions can reflect the covert side of a society.

When we view Disneyland as a cultural mirror, we must be prepared to catch glimpses of ourselves, which do not flatter us; so we turn away from the negative and seek a more positive image of ourselves. It is the negative feedback about our collective selves that may drive us to seek shelter in the ethnocentric illusions we spend so much time creating around us. They can be used, then, to protect us from having to question who and what we are. It comes as no surprise that Disneyland emerged within our culture. It is as much a product of American society and culture as it was a creation of Walt Disney himself. From 1948, when the project first began, to 1955, when it finally opened, Walt Disney was able to sell bankers and the American people an important cultural illusion. Disney was always concerned about the ability to create and sustain illusions (Thomas, 1994). This is why it has become more of a shrine to us and why, perhaps, it is so popular.

Walt Disney knew he was building something that reflected us and our culture. He also knew his concept was good business. He once told French cartoon artists, "Don't go for the avant-garde stuff. Be commercial. What is art, anyway? It's what people like. So give them what they like. There is nothing wrong with being commercial" (Thomas, 1994, p. 277).

Disney's view of the theme park allows us to see how illusions can be fostered through nostalgia, a form of altered historical pasts in the Meadian perspective (see also Kasson, 1978).

"Here [Disneyland] the older generation can recapture the nostalgia of days gone by . . ." He also knew that nostalgia was "corny" but according to Thomas, "He became inured to accusations of corn from critics, from scholars, even from his own children. Once he ran a new Disney film at home and Diane (his daughter) remarked, 'Gee, Dad, that's corny!' Her father replied, 'maybe so, but millions of people eat corn. There must be a reason why they like it so much!'" (Thomas, 1994, p 277).

The illusion of the "Magic Kingdom" is what produced such a great commercial success for Disney. He was able to do this without allowing us to think of it as a business. This is why Disney is such a great illusion maker, for, according to Thomas, illusion was everything for Walt Disney. Thomas describes one incident where an employee, a publicity man, parked his car near Frontier Land railway station. "When people come here, they expect to see the frontier," Walt told him. "Your car destroys the whole illusion. I don't ever want to see a car inside the park again" (Thomas, 1994, p.260).

Main Street and Fantasy Land

The fine line between business and illusion can be seen by how Disney solved the problem of Main Street stores. Again, according to Thomas (1994, p.252), we see a man dedicated to maintaining an illusion for us.

Walt wanted Main Street to be five-eighth scale, creating an air of nostalgic fantasy. But the stores along the street had to be practical ones where people could browse and shop. The art directors found the solution by making the ground floor 90 percent scale, the second floor 80 percent, and the third floor 60 percent. The result was a charming illusion.

The "lands" of Disney comprise the theme park. And it is not by accident that Fantasy Land lies at the center of Disney's creation. In many respects, Fantasy Land represents the American dream, and the American dream lies deep within American culture. It is this dream that allows us to believe that we can accomplish anything if we just work hard (part of the Protestant ethic) and solve problems through technology, and that today's fantasy is really tomorrow's reality. However, the American dream remains only an illusion for many people, and for others, the illusion has been replaced by disillusionment.

This is the problem of basing our perceptions on illusions for when the illusions fail, only disillusionment can take their place. The entire theme of Disney's Fantasy Land is the concept in the song/poem of the Disney character Jiminy Cricket: "When you wish upon a star, makes no difference who you are; when you wish upon a star your dreams come true."

It is this fantasy life that gives the theme park its focus. The castle at the end of Main Street epitomizes that focus. This fantasy theme carries over into the other "lands" as well. We fantasize about life on the Mississippi when we board the Mark Twain steamboat. We fantasize about America at the turn of the century as we go down Main Street. We fantasize about untamed wilderness in Adventure Land. And we can even fantasize about our future. Illusion is everywhere, and we become part of it.

Adventure Land

This is where the untamed wilderness, hostile and beautiful, is viewed. It is also a place where "primitive" cultures reside prior to the introduction of more "advanced" technological societies. This view of primitive cultures is not exclusively an American perspective but one that is generally shared by most western cultures. It was Western cultures that provided the classification system of how cultures are defined. The word *primitive* was first used to distinguish between the more technologically advanced and those based upon hunting and gathering or horticulture. As Western cultures became more industrialized, the newly discovered cultures were measured against how far they stood from the industrial ones. The "natives" with the nose bones in Adventure Land speak to this illusion we have of "primitive" cultures—people with "inferior" cultures to our own "superior" one. Disneyland captures this western cultural bias against nonindustrial societies and fosters the illusion that western culture is better. Part of this illusion goes back to the positive romantic notion of the "noble savage," which has also been a part of our European heritage. It is therefore not surprising to find both primitive and romantic illusions of less technologically advanced cultures in Disneyland, just as we can find them in the larger society as well.

Another important aspect of Adventure Land relates to the illusions we have of nature. Apart from very small children, most adults know they are in an artificial setting when they cruise the African jungle ride. We are provided a glimpse of the hostile environment prior to us changing it through our technology. In fact, we can construct our version of nature almost anywhere, just like the jungle ride at Disneyland. Our cities, parks, shopping malls, and even our theme parks are human-made constructions, where we shape nature to our desires. In many respects, the Adventure Land setting depicts the juxtaposition of nature and humans that can be traced back to Jewish and Christian theology over three thousand five hundred years ago. The idea that nature can be shaped and tamed by God's children (humans) is a deep cultural illusion, which gives us the power to move mountains in his name. On a more practical scale, we now use earth-moving equipment instead of prayer, but the concept is still the same. If a mountain does present a problem, we can now haul it away. If we need a mountain, we build one. This is a message that is reflected to us, not only at Disneyland but also throughout our institutions as well.

There are those who would argue that the human vs. nature concept could hardly be an illusion any longer since we have built an entire civilization and many nations on this belief. However, the illusionary quality of this process can still be observed when we are reminded that nature can "take back" many of our accomplishments through volcanic eruptions, earthquakes, floods, droughts, disease, and similar natural disasters. In fact, many scientific debates now rage over the impact of our approach to nature and how our policies may be detrimental to our continuing as a species on this planet.

The illusion that we can control nature through technology allows us to think we have nature "under control." Our own American history is a march from the Atlantic to the Pacific Ocean, a history validating the illusion as "reality." It is, therefore, not by accident that Frontier Land lies next to Adventure Land in the theme park called Disneyland.

Frontier Land

Americans moving west is the theme of this "land." This small piece of Disneyland real estate represents about two hundred years of American history. The place is ripe with illusions, which run deep in our culture in a variety of ways. The frontier imagery depicted in this area is a composite of illusions we have of frontier America, portrayed by movies, television, novels, and a variety of folktales and other stories, which have emerged in our culture. However, the historical perspective we get from Frontier Land is quite narrow and fits nicely into Mead's notion of the past. Disney has adjusted the past to meet the needs of the present, which gives us the illusion of a tame and uplifting frontier.

> However, America has had a variety of frontiers, which have been reduced to a sort of common western frontier kind of imagery. According to Strauss (1976), even Frederick Turner, a recognized authority on frontier life, has contributed to our somewhat fixed view of a one-dimensional frontier. This view is also supported by Goetzman (1994, p. xiii):

> > Contrary to Turner's hypothesis, the Western experience in the main appears not to have brought distinctiveness as such to bear on the country, but instead offered a theatre in which American patterns of culture could be endlessly mirrored.

What image we do have of ourselves on the frontier is certainly an illusion today, especially as it is depicted at Disneyland. Walt Disney did not formulate his own perception of America's frontier. He was helped by the army of journalists, novelists, artists, photographers, and even historians who have contributed to our collective misperceptions of what the frontier was really like. Disney's success is to capture some of the more popular illusions we have of our past frontier imagery in dramatic fashion and to make these illusions a permanent part of Disneyland itself.

One of the images we have of our past frontier is a place of new beginnings. It was also, unfortunately, a place of endings, especially for the native American population, for it was on the frontier where the native tribes began to view their own demise. It was a place where conflicts were played out: white settlers and native tribes, and yeoman farmers and slave holders. It was a place where even rural interests and urban influences met in ways that began to change the political and economic picture of America forever. Genocide of the native American tribes is not part of the Frontier Land we can view at Disneyland. Disney's frontier is a much happier and joyful place, the illusion of which we tend to enjoy seeing and thinking about as a culture.

Tomorrow Land

Most of Disneyland is past oriented, which is why it is so easy to apply Mead's typology to see how our past becomes shaped into illusions. This particular topic of historical revisionism has been addressed by historians with respect to the film industry (Wilford, 1990; Winkler, 1995).

Tomorrow Land is different. Illusions of what tomorrow will hopefully bring, vis-à-vis new technological innovations, are displayed with pride and optimism (see Tiger, 1979). So while the other lands of Disney reflect our past achievements, Tomorrow Land reflects our future. It is a bright and hopeful future, where technology and science combine to make tomorrow possible. As a culture, we are quick to seek out new technologies to solve current problems, and Tomorrow Land represents a window from which to view these new technologies. Thomas Edison, Henry Ford, the Wright brothers, Alexander Graham Bell, Albert Einstein, Packard and Bell, and Bill Gates are our cultural heroes (Klapp, 1972). The other lands of Disney have become a shrine to our past technological achievements, but Tomorrow Land gives us a glimpse of what future technological marvels may hold for us all.

Space is the new frontier in Disneyland. It is the place where new medicines will be manufactured, new products invented, and new cities are to be built—a future is built upon optimism. We see a way out of our problems of today if we put our faith in technology. Our cities will be more livable, and our ability to communicate with each other will be easier and less costly. Our transportation systems will make traveling quick and easy—without pollution. The illusion of the future becomes more powerful because it is fueled with optimism (Tiger, 1979). It is the combination of optimism and technological innovation, which makes Tomorrow Land an enjoyable place. This can be said for not only Disneyland but also our whole material culture and its values. This is what makes Disneyland so popular. It is a place where the negative side of anything is never revealed, for it would destroy the illusion. This is why we create illusions around us—illusions that alter our views of the past and future so we can live with ourselves in the present.

Cultural Illusions: Beyond Disneyland

Disneyland is a useful metaphor to explore how illusions can emerge within a culture. While Disneyland is designed to create specific illusions, what we get is a way of observing the covert illusions as well. These are the illusions we construct around us so the reality of sociological events does not penetrate too deeply into our thinking. They are, for a better definition, symbolic cocoons, which permit us (and those in the social worlds where we work and live) to be buffered from those ideas and practices that run contrary to how we want to see ourselves, individually and collectively (see Caughey, 1984, for an extensive psychological perspective on this process).

I would like to discuss three examples of illusions, which appear to run deep in our culture. These include the illusions of (1) equality, (2) progress, and (3) perfect government.

1. Equality has been defined in a number of ways throughout our history. Equality of opportunity is the latest expression of this concept. We may not be equally wealthy, but we all have an equal chance to be. This, at least, is one of our ideal objectives as a society. We have, in fact, constructed an extensive and powerful illusion that permits most Anglo-Americans to see the ideal as real. Each generation of white Americans rarely sees a serious gap between the reality of opportunity for African, Latino, and native Americans, especially, and the illusion of attainment. There may be some consensus that the "objective" of racial equality with respect to opportunities may not be fully realized, but certainly it is "close enough" to become the perceived reality by white Americans. This is why Anglo-Americans consistently poll the way they do—by indicating that racial problems have low priority in their perspective. The illusion of equality keeps obscuring and disallows further concern and action. The collective voices that object to such a perspective become only shrill and annoying to those who have become comfortable with the illusion of equality. Even when Anglo-Americans were committing genocide on the frontier (something not mentioned as a topic of discussion in Disneyland), most Americans thought they were doing the right thing by advancing civilization to a race of savages, even if it killed them.

It is interesting to note that one important aspect of equality of opportunity is that it is based upon individual effort. An individual must grab it when it comes along or prepare for it as individuals. I believe this is why we are entertained by the Mountain Man image at Disneyland, for the Mountain Man represents the rugged individualism necessary to capture opportunity. However, there appears to be two views of this person in American history: the first, as depicted by Washington Irving (1985) and the European literary view of Bernard De Voto (1989). The second and probably more realistic view of these people can be found in Billington (1995) and Goetzman (1994). In the first view of the Mountain Man, we see a transition from free trappers to these rugged individuals living on their own. The second image depicts these men as part of the genocide process that most Americans feel uncomfortable in accepting. They were Indian killers and men with political connections, as opposed to the isolated view, which prevails in most American minds when thinking about them. They even used the central government to aid them in their work on the frontier (Goetzman, 1994).

2. Progress seems to be another illusion Americans (and most other cultures as well) use to explain economic growth. We continue to believe that progress, and an expanding economy, is necessary to maintain our standard of living. Progress has come to mean the accelerated use of natural resources by societies all over the world without regard to environmental concerns. Exactly how long we can sustain this illusion before major natural disasters begin to emerge is really the question. We already see some signs of it with regard to the deteriorating environment. Water pollution on a global scale, the ozone depletion of the atmosphere, the hydrocarbon emissions from fossil fuels, the depletion of fossil fuels, the inability to store nuclear waste for ten thousand years, the population growth of the planet, and the global warming, which may cause massive coastal flooding are all examples (Lemonick, 1987; Duvall and Sessions, 1987). Despite all of these warnings, our ecological illusion of progress is quite intact and is kept fueled by our ability to maintain a positive concept of what we do.

We may be seeing some major signs that the illusion of progress is becoming more difficult to sustain. However, living in a consumer culture, we are either forced to maintain the illusion or accept disillusionment in its place. Doing things that may be good for the environment (recycling cans, bottles and paper, conserving water, and driving slower) may actually prolong the illusion of progress before disillusionment gains ground on it. It will certainly be interesting to watch.

3. Americans have always had an interesting relationship with its government. We take great pride in knowing that the American system of government is perfect. Even when we experience periods of disenchantment with those who occupy positions of power within the various branches of government, we still believe that we have perfect government. And political parties and politicians are quite knowledgeable about this aspect of American culture, for they are quite successful in their attempts to sell us what we generally want to hear to maintain the illusion. How else can we explain that elections resemble theater more than a political process? How else can we explain that candidates for political office, in order to be successful, must be attractive, smile a great deal, and not possess any of the human flaws, which most people possess? Does our illusion of perfect government require "perfect" people to run it? We define the "perfect" candidate as someone who looks good on television and not necessarily how their knowledge and experience may solve social problems (Nimmo, 1985; Graber, 1985). Dan Nimmo summarizes the political process. "Any political campaign, and certainly a presidential election campaign, is a continuous exercise in the creation, recreation, and transmission of significant symbols through language, both verbal and nonverbal. It is an enterprise aimed at mobilizing electoral support around a series of attractive, appealing symbols, i.e., a symbolic enterprise" (Nimmo, 1985, p. 31). Doris A. Graber (1985, p.38) gives us another view from the same issue.

   Words are like *Pavlovian cues*—just as animals can be taught to associate the sound of a bell with food, so people are continually conditioned to associate verbal cues with past, direct, and vicarious experiences. Verbal conditioning can be done most effectively through what political linguists call condensation symbols. These are more popularly called code words. Examples are: "The American Way," "racism," "special interests," "rainbow coalition," and yes, "where's the beef?" which hints at disappointed expectations and a lack of substance. Condensation symbols create meanings economically—one phrase or word does it all. The symbol conveys facts, visual images, feelings, and evaluations.

It appears that we are not offended by these practices. As Nimmo (1985, pp.34-38) points out our political institution is theater, and the main choreographer is the media. We are openly manipulated through simple, symbolic images. The same techniques, which are used to sell us hamburgers and cars, are also used to sell us candidates for political office. This is ample evidence that we are not yet disturbed that we are being manipulated. We don't even mind if those who manipulate us know that we know. The illusion of rational decision making on the voters part and the illusion that our political institutions are being served and that candidates believe they stand for important and rational issues are all examples of the power of illusions. Nothing seems to change, our love of illusion appears to be greater than our rational abilities, and perfect government remains intact. However, just as in the other two above examples, there are signs that things may be changing. Voter apathy, militia movements, and political cynicism in general are all examples of disillusionment, and this we should be alert to.

Why We Keep Constructing Illusions

Illusions are possible because humans are subjected to two "illusion principles" during primary socialization. Illusion principle no. 1 is based upon the fact that as biological entities, we need constant monitoring and control by adults to stay alive. Infants remain alive because adults take charge of their nourishment, hygiene, shelter, and comfort needs. The main point is that we emerge from primary socialization with our first and most permanent illusion—the illusion that someone is in control. Illusion principle no. 2 develops when "someone" *should* be in control, especially when control appears to be elusive or not forthcoming. In time, we begin to learn that some portion of that collective "someone" can be us. This could be interpreted as Mead's "generalized other." It is the ability to see the "collective self" as being part of what controls us or what we think controls us. Our reliance upon the illusion of control is what makes the process so powerful. We are always assuming that the portions of society we cannot see or control are "under control." This is really what makes society possible. We can always assume that control is possible and that "someone" is always in control. Both illusion principles are formed during primary socialization and reinforced during secondary as well. By the fact that we emerged from childhood alive makes us vulnerable to illusions since the illusion of control is fixed for life. We can never assume that the world is out of control or we couldn't live in it without going mad. Illusions keep us sane, and therefore, we tend to collectively construct them to insure that the world is in "control." This is why the loss of control over our lives is sometimes more distressing than having a tyrant (or tyrannical structure) controlling us too much.

The problem with illusions is that they make social change very difficult. Why change if the illusion of control is intact? The problem is convincing people that change may be necessary or convincing them that their perception of the situation is really an illusion. Such talk is dismissed, especially if the illusion has become the only way to define reality. This is why it may be better to discuss the social construction of illusion rather than relying on Berger and Luckmann (1967) who define it as reality.

Another problem with relying on illusions to protect us is they are not useful when things change rapidly. In most cases, the only thing that can replace an existing illusion is disillusionment, as was discussed above. Strained, or even shattered, illusions leave us with little or nothing to believe in. Perhaps this is where Durkheim's anomie is most appropriate. We think one way for so long that we are unable to think differently when we have to. We give up and believe that society has left us. Loss of control within our various social worlds may leave our illusions in shambles. Riots, wars, earthquakes, and other natural disasters can render existing social control networks unworkable. Illusions of "someone in control" are exposed, and disillusionment takes its place.

Summary

Humans are constantly constructing illusions that are used to insure that we are in control of our social worlds. They are sometimes constructed in very overt ways, which are demonstrated by the film industry, the theater, the music industry, and theme parks like Disneyland—all obvious examples, where illusion building entertains us. It becomes more of a problem when we begin to build illusions around our social institutions, not for entertainment, but to reassure us that we have our social worlds under control. Since we are born and raised with the illusions of control intact, we find it quite easy to rely on our illusions to protect us from the unknown. We need our illusions to keep us sane; yet they restrict us in our ways of seeing the world differently. Three examples have been presented where the illusion plays a significant role in maintaining current values and social institutions. Other examples could be discussed at length in future articles. Freedom, individuality, sportsmanship, free trade, and justice are sustained by powerful and complex illusions.

We would rather wait until our illusions are shattered completely and until we do something to change them. We can live with strained illusions, and we do it all the time. We change our historical past in ways that suit us (Mead's theory of the past). We are quite capable of creating and maintaining illusions, which we should be studying from a sociological perspective. Let us begin to study this interesting social process and develop a theory of illusion construction.

Bibliography

Chapter One

Abbott, Andrew. *The System of Professions: An Essay on the Division of Expert Labor.* The University of Chicago Press, 1988.

Becker, Howard and E. C. Hughes. *Boys in White.* University of Chicago Press, 1961.

Blau, Peter. *Exchange and Power in Social Life.* New York, Wiley 1964.

Caplow, T. *The Sociology of Work.* University of Minnesota Press, 1964.

Chapoulie , Jean-Michel, "Everett Hughes and the Chicago Tradition," *Sociological Theory*, Vol. 14, 1996.

Duff, Raymond and August Hollingshead, "Dying and Death," *Sickness and Society.* New York, Harper, 1968.

Duke University, "Curriculum Guide and Training Manual for the Pathologists' Assistant," 1970.

Freidson, Eliot. *Profession of Medicine.* Dodd, Mead and Co., 1970.

Goffman, E. *Stigma.* Notes on the Management of Spoiled Identity. Prentiss Hall, Inc. 1963.

Goldberger, N. *The Training of the Funeral Director.* Unpublished paper, Boston College. 1971.

Gross, N. ,W.S. Mason and A.W. McEachern, *Exploration in Role Analysis.* New York, Wiley, 1958.

Hughes, E. C. *Men and Their Work.* Glencoe: The Free Press, 1958.

Schwartz, B. "The Social Psychology of the Gift," *American Journal of Sociology.* V. 73, 1967.

Sudnow, D. *Passing On: The Social Organization of Dying.* Prentice-Hall, 1967.

Thibaut, John and Kelley, Harold, *Social Psychology of Groups.* John Wiley & Sons, Inc., 1959.

Winch, R.F., "The Theory of Complementary Needs In Mate Selection," *American Sociological Review*, Vol. 20, pp. 52-56, 1955.

Yinger, J. Milton. *Toward a Field Theory of Behavior.* McGraw-Hill & Hill Book Co., 1965.

Chapter Two

Becker, Howard, and Anselm Strauss, "Careers, Personality and Adult Socialization," *American Journal of Sociology.* Vol. 62, pp. 253-263., 1975.

Blauner , Robert, *Alienation and Freedom: The Factory Worker and His* Industry, University of Chicago, 1964.

Faulkner, Robert, *Hollywood Studio Musicians,* Chicago, Aldine-Atherton, 1971.

Glaser, Barney editor, *Organizational Careers.* Chicago: Aldine Publishing Company, 1968.

Glaser, Barney and Anselm Strauss, *The Discovery of Grounded Theory*, Weidenfeld and Nicolson, 1968.

Hughes, Everett, *Men and Their Work*, Free Press (Glencoe), 1958. *The Sociological Eye*, Chicago, Aldine-Atherton, 1971.

Nelkin, Dorothy, *On the Season: Aspects of the Migrant Labor System*, The Distribution Center, New York State School of Industrial and Labor Relations , Cornell University, Ithaca, 1970

Roy, Donald F. "Banana Time: Job Satisfaction and Informal Interaction". *Human Organization* **18** (04): 158-168, 1952.

Chapter Three

Benedict, Ruth. *Patterns of Culture*. Houghton. 1958

Black, Herbert. "The Sociology of Gambling," *American Journal of Sociology*, Vol. LVII, No. 3. Nov. 1951.

Faulkner,Robert,*HollywoodStudioMusicians*,Chicago,Aldine-Atherton, 1971.

Geertz, Clifford. "Deep Play: Notes on the Balinese Cockfight," The Interpretation of Culture: Selected Essays. Hutchensen of London, 1964.

Gross, Edward. *Work and Society*. New York: Thomas Y. Crowell, 1958.

Heinrich Böll: *Der Mann mit den Messern*. In: *Heinrich Böll Werke. Romane und Erzählungen* 1. 1947-1952. *Herausgegeben von Bernd Balzer*. Kiepenheuer & Witsch Köln 1977 (ergänzt e Neuaufl. 1987), S. 102-114 (877 Seiten).

Inhaber, Herbert. "Rich with Energy from Conventional and Nonconventional Sources," *Science,* Vol. 203, Feb. 23, 1979.

Janowitz, Morris, *The Professional Soldier: A Social and Political Portrait*, The Free Press, Glencoe, 1960.

Lying, Steven, *American Journal of Sociology*, Vol. 95, pp. 851-856, Jan 1990.

Miller, Elenor, *American Journal of Sociology*, Vol 96, pp. 1530-1539, May, 1991.

Strauss, Anselm. *Negotiation: Varieties, Concepts, Processes, and Social Order*. Jossey-Bass, 1979.

Thorn, Barrie. "Political Activist as Participant Observer: Conflicts of Commitment in a Study of the Draft Resistant Movement of the 1960s," *Contemporary Field Research*, Robert M. Emerson, editor. Waveland Press Inc., Prospect Heights, Illinois, 1983.

Tunstall, Jeremy, *The Fisherman: The Sociology of an Extreme Occupation*, MacGibbon & Kee 1972.

Von Newman, John and Oskar Morgenstern. *Theory of Games and Economic Behavior.* Princeton University Press, first edition, 1944.

Willet, Allan. *The Economic Theory of Risk and Insurance, PHD dissertation*. Columbia University, 1901.

Chapter Four

Faulkner, Robert, "Dilemmas in Commercial Work: Hollywood Film Composers and Their Clients," *Sage Publications*, Inc. 1976.

Goffman, Erving *Asylums*, Chicago, Aldine Publishing Company, 1961.

Roy, Donald F. "Banana Time: Job Satisfaction and Informal Int eracti on". *Human Organization* **18**, No. 4, pp 158-168, Winter 1960.

Strauss, Anselm, *Negotiation: Varieties, Concepts, Processes and Social Order*. Jossey-Bass, 1979.

Chapter Five

Altheide, David. "The Irony of Security." *Urban Life*, Vol. 42, July 1975.

Benveniste, Guy. *The Politics of Expertise*. Berkeley: The Glendessary Press, 1972.

Bilke, Arthur, editor. *Private Security: Standards and Goals from the Official Private Task Force Report*. Washington DC: Government Printing Office, 1976.

Davis, Edward B. Unpublished dissertation. Boston College, 1985.

Faulkner, Robert. *Hollywood Studio Musicians*. Chicago: Aldine-Atherton, 1971.

Goldhamer, Herbert. *The Adviser*. New York: Elsevier North Hollywood, 1978.

Lapin, Jackie. "Whistle While You Work." *California* vol. 12:12. December 1977.

Marchetti and Marks. *CIA and Cult of Intelligence*. New York: Dell Publishing, 1975.

Park, Robert. Society. Chicago: University of Chicago Press, 1952.

Powdermaker, Hortense. *Hollywood: The Dream Factory*. Boston: Little Brown, 1950.

Randell, Richard. *Censorship of the Movies*. Madison, Wisconsin: University of Wisconsin Press, 1968.

Rubinstein, J. *City Police*. New York: Farrar, Strauss, and Sioux, Inc., 1973), p. 47

Rusher, William. "Power of a Critic." San Francisco Chronicle. August 2, 1977.

Sigal, Leon V. *Reporters and Officials: The Organization and Politics of Newsmaking.* DC Heath and Co., 1973.

Sigelman, Lee. "Reporting the News: An Organizational Analysis." *American Journal of Sociology.* Vol. 79.

Spander, Art. "An Official NBA Problem." San Francisco Chronicle. December 13, 1977.

Talese, Gay. *The Kingdom and the Power.* Garden City, New York: Elsevier North Hollwood, 1978.

Wolff, Kurt H., translator and editor. *The Sociology of Georg Simmel.* New York: The Free Press, 1964.

Chapter Seven

Abbott, Andrew. *The System of Professions: An Essay on the Division of Expert Labor.* The University of Chicago Press, 1988.

Cleary, Daniel. "European Universities in Transition." *Science.* Vol. 271, Feb. 1996, pp. 681-701.

Hofstadter, Richard and Wilson Smith. *American Higher Education,* Vol. 1, 1961, The University of Chicago Press.
Ritzer, George. *The McDonaldization of Society,* Thousand Oaks. Fine Forge Press. 1993

Chapter Eight

Berger, Peter and Thomas Luckmann. 1967. *Social Construction of Reality: A Treatise in the Sociology of Knowledge.* Doubleday.

Billington, Ray Allen. 1995. *The Far Western Frontier, 1830-1860.* University of New Mexico Press.

Caughey, John L. 1984. *Imaginary Social Worlds.* University of Nebraska Press.

Devall, Bill and George Sessions. 1987. *Deep Ecology: Living As If Nature Mattered.* Gibbs Smith Publishing.

De Voto, Bernard A. 1989. *The Course of Empire.* Houghton Mifflin.

Graber, Doris A. 1985. "Magical Words and Plain Campaigns." *Society.* V22, No. 4, pp. 38-44.

Goetzman, William H. 1994. *Exploration and Empire: The Explorer and the Scientist in the Winning of the American West.* Texas State Historical Association.

Irving, Washington. 1985. *A Tour on the Prairies.* University of Oklahoma Press.

Kasson, John F. 1978. *Amusing the Million: Coney Island at the Turn of the Century.* Hill and Wang.

Klapp, Orrin E. 1972. *Heroes, Villains and Fools: The Changing American Character.* Aegis Publishing Co.

Lemonick, Michael D. 1987. "Shrinking Shores." *Time.* Aug. 10, pp. 37-47.

Maines, David, N. Sugre, and M. Katovich. 1983. "The Sociological Import of G. H. Mead's Theory of the Past." *American Sociological Review.* 48, pp. 161-173.

Nimmo, Dan. 1985 "Elections as Ritual Drama." *Society.* V. 22, No.4, pp. 31-37.

Schwartz, Barry. 1991 "Social Change and Collective Memory." *American Sociological Review.* 56 April, pp. 221-236.

Strauss, Anselm. 1976. *Images of the American City.* Transaction Publishing.

Thomas, Bob. 1994. *Walt Disney: An American Original.* Hyperion.

Tiger, Lionel. 1979. *Optimism: The Biology of Hope*. Simon and Schuster.

Wilford, John N. 1990. "Anthropology Seen as Father of Maori Lore." *The New York Times*. Feb. 20:C1-3.

Winkler, Karen J. 1995. "History in Hollywood: The Way Films Present the Past." *The Chronicle of Higher Education*. Vol. XLII, No. 16:A10.

Index

Endnotes

Endnotes for Introduction

1. This was also mentioned by Harold Wilensky in his review of Hughes's publication of *Men and Their Work* in 1959. Wilensky notes, "On the universality of standards of work beyond successful conclusion of the task: 'The quack, defined functionally and not in evaluative terms, is the man who continues through time to please his customers but not his colleagues' (p.98). On occupations requiring guilty knowledge: 'The priest cannot mete out penance without becoming an expert on sin.' On professionalism: 'In the purest case the professional would do work which he alone can do, and the work would be a kind wanted everywhere by all men; a maximum of specific bounding would be matched by a maximum of universality' (p. 162)."

2. Abbott, pp. 195-196.

3. Ibid., pp. 29-30.

4. Ibid., p. 55.

5. Ibid., p. 75.

6. Ibid., p. 76.

7. Ibid., p. 57.

8. Faris, p. 111.

9. Jean-Michel Chapoulie's 1996 article on Hughes in *Sociological Theory* provides us with Hughes's research perspective and methodology. "The studies [at Chicago between 1940 and 1960] that depend most clearly on Hughes's program are based almost entirely on intensive fieldwork, generally including observation *in situ* and interviews with populations of a limited size: a particular category of workers in an organization, a particular situation, or a specific occupation" (Vol. 14, Issue 1, March

1996, p. 17). All of the papers contained in this present volume reflect Hughes's research approach as described above.

Endnotes for Chapter One

Suffolk County
Boston City Hospital
Boston, Massachusetts

To Whom It May Concern

This will introduce Mr. Edward Davis, MA, who is a graduate student and teaching Fellow in Sociology at Boston College. Mr. Davis is [a] member of a seminar of mine devoted to the study of the career problems of people in some of the less well-known occupations. He would like to study by observation the work of the morgue attendants. His interest is in them, their careers, their behavior and their problems.

We have found in many work systems such as the health and educational systems, there are quite a number of more or less unseen kinds of work to be done. For the full understanding of these institutions we believe it desirable to learn what we can about these less well-known and less prestigeful occupations and the people in them.

When people go out to do this kind of sociological study they understand fully that they are not to intrude themselves in any way, and that they are to keep very confidential any names or other marks of identification. Our aim is scientific description and analysis of organizations. We find our graduate students and other such investigators very conscientious and trustworthy. In the course of the last several years I have had many students and younger colleagues who have studied medical schools, hospitals, clinics and other institutions very successfully. I am sure Mr. Davis will live up to the professional code of sociology.

Any courtesy shown to him will be greatly appreciated.

Sincerely yours,
Everett C. Hughes

This is the letter of introduction Dr. Hughes provided for me for this project. I'm sure it is similar to the letters he wrote for his students studying work at the University of Chicago.

10 I have discovered that those occupations closest to the death have more stigma attached to their occupational roles than those that deal with the dead at a distance. For example, the diener, funeral director, and hearse driver must be able to deal with verbal and nonverbal stigmatic abuses more than the gravedigger, casket maker, or cemetery caretaker. It's just as if a dead body generates emotional rings in a shock-wave pattern with stigma generated from the "center" or physical nearness to the death and working out to the furthest occupations such as florist and vault (grave liner) placement men.

11 For a complete discussion of this procedure, see Duff and Hollinghead. "Dying and Death." *Sickness and Society,* pp. 306-330.

12 Becker, Hughes, et al. *Boys in White,* p. 224.

13 Barry Schwartz. "The Social Psychology of the Gift." *American Journal of Sociology.* V. 73, No. 1, 1967.

14 Ibid., p. 3.

15 Ibid., p. 4.

16 Hughes. *Men and Their Work,* p. 73.

17 Freidson. *Profession of Medicine,* p. 50.

18 Such occupations in the work system include ambulance drivers, pathologists, dieners, funeral directors, embalmers, hearse drivers, funeral and wake attendants, restorative specialists, teaching and training personnel for embalmers and funeral directors, booking personnel in hospitals, casket makers, casket delivery men, embalming fluid machine companies, casket salesmen, casket designers, funeral clothes manufacturers, cremators, cremator equipment companies and salesmen, cemetery directors, cemetery caretakers, grave diggers, monument designers, cutters and delivery personnel, vault or grave liner companies and delivery

men, florists, religious personnel, newspaper obituary personnel, public executors, insurance companies, death records, plus all of the secretaries and maintenance personnel associated with the above. Even though all of these occupations are concerned directly with death, each one has different phases, career contingencies, and favorite clients, and each career has a distinct identity among themselves and to the society in general.

19   Goldberger. "The Training of the Funeral Director," unpublished.

20   During my exposure with death occupations, I have noticed that each has some form of humor concerning aspects of death. Some people working in hospital booking departments ask the floor nurse, "Has the spoiled meat been removed?" Hearse drivers have jokes concerning the weight and size of the body. Pathologists have been known to describe their role in medicine as "weighing the meat the butcher sends down." Morticians refer to the cremator as the "chef." I would imagine all death occupations are constantly making jokes about death, especially that phase in the work system that they are directly associated with. At the present time, there has been no research in this area.

21   "Curriculum Guide and Training Manual for the Pathologists Assistant," p. 1.

22   Ibid., p. 7.

23   These sixteen to twenty hours has to come in stages since the microscopic slides take just one week to prepare. By the time the resident or pathologists' assistant gets around to reading the slides, the entire procedure can draw out to a month.

24   See W. I. Thomas' Social Behavior and Personality.

25   E. C. Hughes. *Men and Their Work*, p. 77.

26   J. M. Yinger. *Toward a Field Theory of Behavior*, p. 110.

27   Ibid., p. 117.

28   Ibid., p. 103.

29   Ibid., p. 115.

30   Ibid., p. 117, Gross, Mason and Mc Eachern. *Exploration in Role Analysis: Studies in School Superintendents Role*, p. 31.

31   Peter Blau. *Exchange and Power in Social Life*, New York, Wiley, 1964, chapter 6.

32   R. F. Winch. *American Sociological Review*, 1955, p. 20, pp. 52-56.

33   Thibault and Kelley, chapter 7.

34   Ibid.

35   Yinger, p. 119.

36   Thibaut and Kelley, p. 236.

37   Freidson, *Profession of Medicine*, p. 180.

Endnotes for Chapter Two

[38] Glaser, Barney, 1976. *The Patsy and the Subcontractor*. New Brunswick, NJ: Transaction Books.

Endnotes for Chapter Three

[39] Thorne, Barrie. "Political Activist as Participant Observer: Conflicts of Commitment in a Study of the Draft Resistance Movement of the 1960s," pp. 216-234 in *Contemporary Field Research*, Robert M. Emerson, editor, Waveland Press, Inc., Prospect Heights, IL, 1983.

[40] Willett, Allan. *The Economic Theory of Risk and Insurance*, p. 21.

[41] Morgenstern and Von Newman. *Theory of Games and Economic Behavior.*

[42] Strauss, Anselm. *Negotiations: Varieties, Contexts, Processes and Social Order.* Jossey-Bass, 1978.

[43] Gross, Edward. *Work and Society*, p. 198.

[44] Benedict, Ruth. *Patterns of Culture*. Houghton-Muffin, 1958.

[45] Inhaber, Herbert. "Risk with Energy from Conventional and Nonconventional Sources." *Science*. Vol. 203, 23 Feb. 1979.

[46] Prior to publication of this book, the world was once again introduced to the risks associated with a mining career. The trapped Chilean miners in 2010 became a dramatic example of the how risk can be shared on a global scale.

[47] Block, Herbert. "The Sociology of Gambling." *American Journal of Sociology.* Vol. LVII, No. 3, Nov. 1951, p. 218.

[48] Geertz, Clifford. "Deep Play: Notes on a Balinese Cockfight," in *The Interpretation of Culture: Selected Essays*, 16. Hutchinson of London, 1964.

[49] Strauss, Anselm. *Professions, Work, and Careers*. Transaction Publishers, 1975.

Endnotes for Chapter Six

[50] Davis, Fred. "The Cab Driver and His Fare"

[51] Goffman, Erving. 1963. *Behavior in Public Places*. New York: Free Press.

[52] Becker, Howard. 1982. *The Art World*. Berkeley: University of California Press.

[53] Glaser, Barney. 1976. *The Patsy and the Subcontractor*. New Brunswick, NJ: Transaction Books.

Endnotes for Chapter Seven

54   For a complete discussion on jurisdictional disputes see Andrew Abbot, *The System of Profession: An Essay on the Division of Expert Labor*. The University of Chicago Press, 1988. See also "European Universities in Transition," *Science*, Vol. 271, pp. 681-701, 1996.

55   Hofstadter, Richard and Wilson Smith. *American Higher Education*, Vol. 1. The University of Chicago Press, 1961.

Made in the USA
San Bernardino, CA
29 August 2015